RADAR OBSERVES THE WEATHER

LOUIS J. BATTAN was born in 1923 in New York City. After having entered the City College of New York, he enlisted in the U. S. Army Air Force in World War II and later became a weather officer. With a group of selected Air Force lieutenants, he attended radar and electronics classes at Harvard and M.I.T. and was trained in the use of radar equipment for making special meteorological observations. Following the war, he returned to his studies. In 1946, he received his B.S. from New York University and joined the U. S. Weather Bureau where he worked for three years on the Thunderstorm Project, a research program. Graduate work at the University of Chicago resulted in an M.S. degree in 1949 and a Ph.D. in 1953. He remained there after graduation and continued his work on the physics of clouds and precipitation.

In 1958, Dr. Battan joined the staff of The University of Arizona in Tucson as a Professor of Meteorology and the Associate Director of the Institute of Atmospheric Physics. Since then he has continued to do research in the various areas of physical meteorology, including the effects of cloud seeding. Elected in 1959 to the Council of the American Meteorological Society, Professor Battan has served on the Committee on Radar Meteorology, is currently on the Committees on Severe Storm and Cloud Physics, and is an associate editor of the *Journal of the Atmospheric Sciences*, formerly the *Journal of Meteorology*. He is the author of *Radar Meteorology* (University of Chicago Press, 1959), the first textbook to deal with this field, and many articles for scientific journals. Another book by Dr. Battan in the Science Study Series is *The Nature of Violent Storms*, published in 1961.

Radar
Observes the Weather

LOUIS J. BATTAN

SCIENCE
STUDY
SERIES
O

Published by Anchor Books
Doubleday & Company, Inc.
Garden City, New York

ILLUSTRATIONS BY KENNETH CROOK
TYPOGRAPHY BY SUSAN SIEN

THE SCIENCE STUDY SERIES

The Science Study Series offers to students and to the general public the writing of distinguished authors on the most stirring and fundamental topics of science, from the smallest known particles to the whole universe. Some of the books tell of the role of physics in the world of man, his technology and civilization. Others are biographical in nature, telling the fascinating stories of the great discoverers and their discoveries. All the authors have been selected both for expertness in the fields they discuss and for ability to communicate their special knowledge and their own views in an interesting way. The primary purpose of these books is to provide a survey within the grasp of the young student or the layman. Many of the books, it is hoped, will encourage the reader to make his own investigations of natural phenomena.

The Series, which now offers topics in all the sciences and their applications, had its beginning in a project to revise the secondary schools' physics curriculum. At the Massachusetts Institute of Technology during 1956 a group of physicists, high school teachers, journalists, apparatus designers, film producers, and other specialists organized the Physical Science Study Committee, now operating as a part of Educational Services Incorporated, Watertown, Massachusetts. They pooled their knowledge and experience toward the design and creation of aids to the learning of physics. Initially their effort was supported by the National Science Foundation, which has continued to aid the program. The Ford Foundation, the Fund for the Advancement of Education, and the Alfred P. Sloan Foundation have also given support. The Committee has created a textbook, an extensive film series, a laboratory guide, especially designed apparatus, and a teacher's source book.

The Series is guided by a Board of Editors consisting of Bruce F. Kingsbury, Managing Editor; John H. Durston, General Editor; Paul F. Brandwein, the Conservation Foundation and Harcourt, Brace & World, Inc.; Francis L. Friedman, Massachusetts Institute of Technology; Samuel A. Goudsmit, Brookhaven National Laboratory; Philippe LeCorbeiller, Harvard University; and Gerard Piel, *Scientific American.*

PREFACE

Progress in most fields of knowledge is usually made in a stepwise fashion. Periods of slow advance are suddenly followed by periods of rapid surges. Frequently a surge has been brought about by a single discovery or by the development of a new idea or instrument. In the field of physics, for example, the invention of the cyclotron led to rapid advances in nuclear physics. In meteorology the development of a balloon-borne instrument that could telemeter back pressure, temperature, and humidity information led to an explosive advancement in our knowledge of the atmosphere. In more recent years the high-speed electronic computer has revolutionized almost all fields of scientific research (including meteorology).

The introduction of radar has led to a tremendous step forward in cloud and rainfall observations. Since the end of the war, when military radar was turned to peaceful uses, we have learned a great deal about almost all types of weather. Improved weather-observing radars have been built for use on the ground and in the air.

The purpose of this short book is to introduce students and laymen to radar and to acquaint them with its applications as a weather-observing instrument.

An attempt has been made to avoid the use of highly technical terms or phrases in order to make the material easily understood by people with little or no training in science. Readers interested in a more thorough treatment of the subject are referred to a book entitled *Radar Meteorology*, by the same author, which has been published by the University of Chicago Press.

The units of measure employed in this book, or, for that matter, in most current books dealing with science, may be a little confusing to the layman. It is common practice to use various types of units. For example, in English-speaking countries temperatures at the earth's surface are measured in degrees Fahrenheit while temperatures in the free atmosphere are measured in degrees Centigrade. Also, in some places distances are measured in miles, feet, and inches while in others, kilometers, meters and centimeters are the standard units. The use of several systems is recognized as undesirable by most scientists and engineers. Unfortunately, it is difficult to change habits many centuries old. There is a trend toward the universal adoption of the metric system, but the change will be made very slowly. In the meantime, it is necessary to be able to convert from one set of units to another. The Appendix at the end of this book gives information to permit easy conversions.

The author wishes to thank Mr. Morgan Monroe of The University of Arizona for his encouragement and Mr. John H. Durston for his excellent suggestions.

LOUIS J. BATTAN

CONTENTS

RADAR OBSERVES THE WEATHER

CHAPTER 1

INTRODUCTION

In the cockpit of an airliner the pilot is quietly calculating the best course of action. The airplane is engulfed in a heavy cloud mass. The wing tips are not even visible, but periodically one can see a red glow caused by the blinking lights on the wing tips.

Thirty minutes ago the air had been smooth, but now the situation is rapidly becoming unpleasant. At frequent intervals the airplane bounces and shakes, indicating increasingly turbulent conditions. The seat belt sign is on. Every so often flashes of lightning light up the sky.

Some of the passengers who have flown a great deal are listening to the sounds of the engines and mentally flying the airplane. They reduce the air speed to minimize the effects of the air gusts and strain their eyes staring into the mist to see if they can spot the thunderstorms buried in the clouds. The cloud droplets and poor visibility are no cause for alarm. The danger is concentrated in the thunderstorms, where updrafts or downdrafts of several thousand feet per minute are waiting to lift or drop the airplane like a leaf and shake it violently—where hail-stones and lightning are also waiting to strike.

Not many years ago even the good pilots feared the thunderstorm, but now the situation has changed. Yesterday's aviator had to rely on experience and luck to get him through without giving himself and the passengers a good scare. The biggest problem was to locate the thunderstorm regions which harbored the severe weather. When the aircraft is in clouds, it is impossible to see these regions. Today we have a gadget which can "see" through clouds. The pilot of today's airliner has, as part of his flying aids, a radar set which can spot thunderstorms far out ahead of him.

As the airplane penetrates a wall of clouds and moves closer to the region of treacherous weather, the pilot sees it mapped out on a radarscope. After watching for a short time, he can calculate his best course of action. Should he go straight ahead and pick his way between storms by making only slight deviations in airplane heading? Should he begin a long swing around the storm area? Now that he knows where the storms are he can answer these questions. As a result, airplane travel has become safer and, of course, much more comfortable. And the equipment known as radar not only has been an aid to airline travel but has become a standard observational instrument at many weather stations and is used extensively by weather scientists.

What is radar? How does it work? What can it do to improve weather observations? What can it tell us about the ways of the atmosphere?

The word radar came from the term "radio detection and ranging," that is, the use of radio waves to detect objects and to measure the distances to them. Without doubt, radar was one of the outstanding electronic developments that came out of World War II.

Quite clearly, it was of the utmost importance during the war to be able to accurately locate and track enemy airplanes and ships in all types of weather and at any time, day or night. For bombing from airplanes it was essential to be able to locate targets hidden under layers of clouds. Tremendous efforts were devoted to the development of a system which could accomplish these purposes.

Early in the war, in England and other countries under frequent air attacks, widespread use was made of powerful search lights which would seek airplanes in the sky. Although this scheme was quite useful on nights with clear skies, it was a failure when the sky was covered with clouds or when fogs and haze shrouded the ground. Sound ranging techniques also had been used for locating aircraft, but they had many disadvantages. Sound travels at speeds of only about 700 mph and is subject to many deviations in speed and direction by the atmosphere. Sound equipment is still used for detecting underwater vehicles such as submarines, but for aircraft it has been completely abandoned.

For detection of objects on the earth's surface or in the air, radar is far superior to the visual or acoustical methods. It can function over a large range of conditions. It makes no difference whether it is day or night, and ordinary clouds and fog usually do not seriously affect radar. If one wishes, it is possible to detect targets at very great distances as well as very close ones. For these reasons, radar was used extensively during the last war in nearly all phases of ground, naval, and air operations. Since then more powerful and versatile equipment has been built.

Weather Detection

The radar sets employed in World War II were subject to one serious environmental problem. When heavy rain fell between the radar sets and the target, the radar lost some of its effectiveness. If an airplane being tracked with certain types of radar flew into or behind a region of heavy rain, its signal was lost in the echo from the rain or disappeared completely. When ordinary non-raining clouds were present, these effects were usually negligible.

The rainstorms which appeared as strong echoes on the radarscope were a great annoyance to military radar operators. They were a form of "noise" drowning out the important signals. But to meteorologists the noise was music. For the first time it became possible to locate rainstorms, measure their sizes, and watch them grow and move. No longer was it necessary to look at a distant thunderstorm and estimate its distance and speed of movement. Estimation was replaced by measurement! As a result, a large group of meteorological problems became amenable to scientific exploration.

With the introduction of radar, short-term weather

forecasting took a leap forward. One of the important questions facing an airport meteorologist during thunderstorm conditions is, "Will a thunderstorm move over the particular airfield, and if it does, how strong will the wind and rain be and how long will the storm last?" An accurate answer to this question even thirty minutes before a thunderstorm strikes is of great importance. This much time is sufficient to move airplanes into hangars or tie them down and to secure objects which may be blown into airplanes or buildings.

As will be seen later, thunderstorms do not always move with the wind. Consequently, unless one can watch their movements and see them growing, accurate forecasts are almost impossible to make. The only way to obtain the necessary observations is with a suitable radar set. Of course, this is only one way in which radar has been of value to weathermen.

Since the middle forties, when meteorologists began to exploit radar, much new information about the processes of formation of all kinds of clouds and precipitation has been compiled. Today the airlines, private weather companies, and the military and national weather services all use radar. Regions of severe weather such as the so-called "tornado alley" in the central United States and the regions of high hurricane frequency along the Gulf and Atlantic coasts are dotted with radar stations. Violent storms are detected early and tracked across the country. Warnings are issued, and the savings in life and property have paid for the cost of the equipment many times over.

In later sections these aspects of radar meteorology
will be covered in some detail.

Before discussing the applications of radar, however, it is appropriate to examine how radar works
and why it detects droplets of water and ice. The next
few chapters will examine these questions.

CHAPTER 2

PRINCIPLES OF RADAR

Some radar sets are quite weak and emit less power than is used in an ordinary light bulb. Others are so powerful that for very short periods of time the power transmitted could light up an entire town. But in principle they are much the same. They all contain a transmitter, a receiver, an antenna, and an indicator. We shall return to a description of these components, but before doing that, let us see how radar measures the distance to any object, for example, an airplane.

The radar set sends out a pulse of energy in the direction of the airplane (Fig. 1). A small fraction of the energy is reflected back and is detected by the radar. If one knows the speed at which the pulse travels and the time elapsed between transmission and reception of the pulse, one can easily calculate the distance to the airplane. In all radar sets the pulse of energy is in the form of electromagnetic waves, which for most practical purposes can be considered to move at a constant velocity equal to 186,000 miles/sec (3×10^8 meters/sec). Some readers will immediately recognize that this is the velocity of light.

But since light waves also are electromagnetic waves, it should not be unexpected that they move at this speed. To be exact, it has been found that in the atmosphere the electromagnetic, or radio waves, as they are sometimes called, travel slower than light waves but only by a quite small amount.

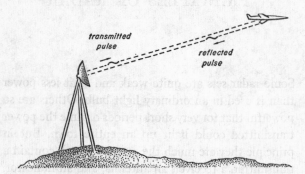

FIG. 1. *A pulse of radar energy travels from the radar set to the airplane and back again at a speed of* 3×10^8 *meters/sec. Dividing time of round trip by two, one can calculate the distance to the airplane.*

Let us return to the example. If the airplane were 20 miles away, the time required for the reflected pulse to return to the radar set would be 40/186,000 or 0.000215 sec. It is common, when short times are involved, to measure the time in microseconds, or millionths of a second. Of the total time of 215 microseconds, 107.5 were consumed as the pulse traveled from the radar set to the target and the other 107.5 were spent as the pulse traveled back again. A radar operator knowing these times could easily calculate that the airplane was 20 miles away.

Of course, with practical radar sets it is not necessary to actually measure the elapsed times. Instead, radarscopes are used to display the location of the target relative to the radar set. Of the large variety

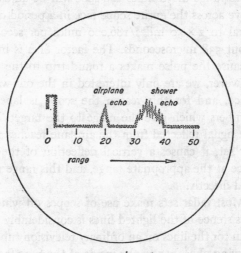

FIG. 2. *A-scope.*

of scopes used one of the simplest is called an A-scope. It is illustrated in Fig. 2. This scope is a tube similar in design to a television picture tube, but instead of having many closely spaced horizontal lines which combine to form a picture, this tube has only one line. It is formed by a beam of electrons impinging on the face of the tube and causing it to glow. The beam begins to move horizontally when the transmitter sends out the pulse. Some of the transmitted energy causes a deflection of the spot to produce the so-called "main bang." The rate at which the spot moves across the scope face is adjusted so that a particular horizontal displacement corresponds to a certain range to the target. On a scope designed to present information about targets out to a maximum range of 50 miles the spot will be adjusted to move across the entire scope face in a period of time equal to 2×50 miles/186,000 miles per second, or about 538 microseconds. The factor of 2 is inserted because the pulse makes a round trip to the target. However, we are only interested in the one-way distance, and for this reason the scope is labeled in numbers which give the range to the target. When the signal reflected from the airplane reaches the radar set, it causes a vertical deflection of the scope trace at the appropriate range, and this range can be read directly.

Most radar sets make use of scopes on which the persistence of the lighted lines is considerably higher than for the lines on an ordinary television tube. The glowing phosphor on the inside of the tube face is of a type that, once it is illuminated, can glow for an appreciable part of a second. This property of the radarscope makes it easier to see the deflections.

A radarscope such as the one illustrated in Fig. 2 gives us more information than the distance to the target. The vertical amplitude of the returned signal, or echo as it is usually called, depends on the strength of the echo. When the echo is weak, the airplane pip, for example, is short. When the signal is strong, the airplane pip is tall. When one is primarily interested in detecting airplanes, this feature of the radarscope may not be too important, but when one begins to examine rainstorms it becomes very important. As we shall see later, the amplitude of the echo can be used to estimate rainfall intensity.

Types of Scopes

Various other types of scopes are used on weather radars. The most common is the plan-position indi-

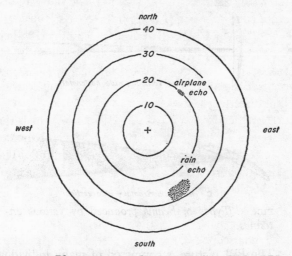

FIG. 3. *Plan-position indicator, usually called a PPI.*

cator, commonly called the PPI. As the name implies, this scope presents a plan view of the echoes, that is, the view one would see if he could look down on the entire picture. Fig. 3 shows a PPI with the echo from an airplane and a small rain shower. As you can see, this type of presentation allows one to read off not only the range to the target but the bearing as well. An airplane is located at a range of 20 miles and a bearing of 45 degrees.

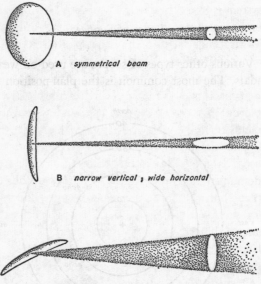

A symmetrical beam

B narrow vertical ; wide horizontal

C narrow horizontal ; wide vertical

FIG. 4. *Types of beams produced by various antennas.*

The PPI picture is composed of many individual traces formed as the spot of light moves from the center of the tube to the outside edge, returns very rapidly to the center, and repeats the procedure as the trace turns around the circle in synchronism with the scanning of the radar antenna. In order to understand how a radar set is capable of obtaining bearing information, it is necessary to examine the role played by the antenna.

Radar sets can be constructed with an antenna of the type used in a television system, but it would not have much application. Since the aim of a television system is to reach as many people as possible, the energy transmitted is usually sent out in all directions. With a radar set, on the other hand, one wishes to concentrate the energy into a narrow beam. For this purpose metal reflectors, similar in shape to the mirror reflectors used in large searchlights, are often employed. The exact shape of the antenna reflector depends on the aim of the radar engineer. See Fig. 4. If one wishes a narrow, pencil-shaped beam, he can use a large concave metal dish. In some cases it is desirable to have a beam that is narrow in the vertical plane but wide in the horizontal plane. The reflector for such a beam looks like a banana peel with the largest dimensions in the same plane as the narrow-beam width. In general, the larger the antenna, the smaller the beam within which the radar energy is concentrated.

The antenna of a radar set with a PPI rotates around a vertical axis in a smooth fashion. As the antenna rotates, the beam of light extending from the center of the PPI to the outer edge rotates in synchronism with it. When the antenna is pointing at 30 degrees, the scope trace also points toward 30 degrees. If the beam produced by the antenna is narrow, let us say 1 degree, one can spot airplanes and other targets with precision. As the antenna beam sweeps over the target, echoes will be obtained only when the beam is pointing at the target.

The utility of the PPI for weather observations can easily be imagined. For example, rain showers and other types of weather can be detected and the location noted.

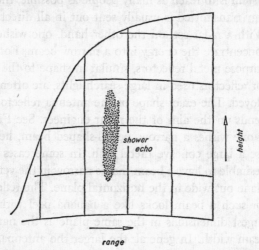

FIG. 5. *Range-height indicator, usually called an RHI.*

Another type of scope in common use is the range-height indicator, called the RHI. As can be seen in Fig. 5, this scope gives a plot of the echo height versus range. It should be noted that the term *range* means the straight-line distance to the target. If the radar beam is pointing horizontally, the range and horizontal distance are equal. On the other hand, if the target is a high-flying airplane, the range can be much larger than the horizontal distance. See Fig. 6. In order to obtain a range-height presentation, the radar antenna scans in the vertical plane. As it rocks up and down, the beam on the scope rocks up and down and paints a picture of the echoes. The RHI is employed when one is concerned with direct readings of the altitudes of targets. Meteorologists frequently use it for measuring the heights of thunderstorms.

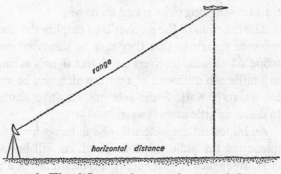

FIG. 6. *The difference between horizontal distance and range to an airplane.*

We pointed out earlier that with an A-scope the strength of the echo can be measured by noting the vertical amplitude of the echoes. On PPI- and RHI-scopes the echo intensity is related to the brightness of the echo. The stronger the returned signal, the brighter will be the echo, at least up to the point where the radar system becomes *saturated*. This is a signal level above which the system can do no more than indicate that the saturation level has been reached.

Although radar transmitters emit very powerful signals, the amount of power reflected and received from weather targets usually is quite small. For example, many radar sets transmit powers of 100 kilowatts or more. As already noted, this is in the form of short pulses which are relatively wide apart in time. A typical radar set may transmit pulses of one microsecond duration spaced at intervals of 1000 microseconds. This relatively long period is allowed for the reflected signals to return to the radar receiver before the next outgoing pulse is sent on its way.

The function of the receiver is to amplify the small reflected signals so that they may be displayed on a scope. Most radar receivers can detect signals as small as a millionth millionth of a watt, which may be written as 10^{-12} watt. Some sets are sensitive enough to detect as little as 10^{-14} watt.

An important characteristic of a radar set is the frequency of the radio waves involved. As will be seen later, frequency is particularly important when a radar set is used for observing clouds and rain. In general, the higher the frequency the smaller the droplets which the radar can detect. For weather observations frequencies higher than 30,000,000,000 cycles per second and as low as 1,500,000,000 cps have been employed. Since the speed of radio waves can be considered to be constant and is given by the equation *speed equals frequency times wave length*, each radio frequency corresponds to a particular wave length. Knowing that the speed of the radio waves is 3×10^{10} centimeters per second, one can easily calculate that radar sets used in weather work cover the range from about 1 to 20 cm. The choice of wave length depends on the aim of the investigator. If he wishes to detect small water droplets, the short wave lengths are best. If the aim is to examine widespread rainstorms, longer wave lengths are more desirable. The reasons for these statements will become evident in the following chapters.

Radar Sets Used for Weather Observations

Some radar sets are very large with hundreds of tubes and are so complicated that squadrons of men

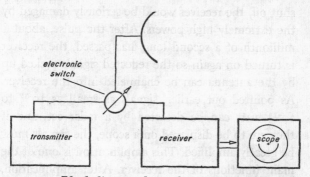

FIG. 7. *Block diagram shows the major components of a radar set.*

are needed to "keep them on the air." Others are relatively simple and can be maintained easily by one technician. The complexity of the radar depends on various factors such as the wave length, the transmittal power, the antenna size, and the types and number of scopes.

The basic design of all conventional radar sets may be represented by the block diagram given in Fig. 7. Incidentally, it is called a *block diagram* because major components are represented merely as blocks without any of the details shown.

The heart of the radar set is the transmitter, which produces the pulses of electromagnetic waves. Most radar sets used in meteorology have pulse powers ranging from about 25 to as high as 500 kilowatts. After the pulse is produced, the energy is passed on to the antenna, which radiates it in a narrow beam. During the transmitting period the receiver is effectively shut off by the *electronic switch*. If it were not shut off, the receiver would be seriously damaged by the extremely high powers. After the pulse, about 1 millionth of a second long, has passed, the receiver is turned on again so the reflected signals picked up by the antenna can be channeled into the receiver. As pointed out earlier, signals as small as 10^{-12} to 10^{-14} watt can be detected by a radar set, and if they are to be displayed on a scope, the signals must be greatly amplified. This amplification is one of the main functions of the receiver. After amplification, the signals are channeled to one or more scopes, which produce the echoes which are of so much interest.

In the middle forties meteorologists used surplus military radar sets for making weather observations. One of the sets first employed was called the SCR-584. It was a 10-cm radar whose antenna was mounted on the roof of a trailer. Because of its great versatility, the SCR-584 had an illustrious military career. Among the jobs it accomplished were the detection and tracking of enemy airplanes, the control of our own airplanes when engaged in bombing activities over nearby enemy positions, and the control of antiaircraft guns. The first weather function it served was to obtain measurements of winds aloft by tracking a radar target fastened to a balloon. Knowing the track of the balloon, the observers found it a simple matter to calculate the winds.

Other military radar sets used widely in the weather services are known as the AN/APQ-13 and the AN/APS-2F.* Both were originally designed for purposes of airborne navigation and bombing. Except for the fact that the first is a 3-cm set and the latter a 10-cm set, the two radar sets are similar in most respects. Both produce fairly low powers, about 40 kilowatts, and have antennas about 30 inches in diameter.

A military radar set that has been employed for many research jobs by meteorologists is the AN/TPS-10 shown in Plate I. It is a 3-cm, vertically scanning radar. The vertical dimension of the antenna is about 3 meters and the horizontal width about 1 meter. This antenna produces vertical and horizontal beam widths of 0.7 and 2.0 degrees, respectively. As would be expected, this radar set presents the echoes on an RHI of the type illustrated in Figs. 5 and 6.

* The designations given radar equipment are coded symbols used to make the equipment easily identifiable. For example, AN/APS stands for Army (A), Navy (N), Airborne (A), Radar (P), Search (S). Thus AN/APS-2F means that the equipment is an airborne search radar model 2F.

Since 1950 two radar sets have been designed and constructed for the weather service. The first, called the AN/CPS-9 (Plate II), came out about 1951. It was designed by the Air Force and used to replace the old AN/APQ-13 sets in weather stations all over the world. The so-called CPS-9 is a 3-cm set with a circular antenna about 2.4 meters in diameter and is capable of scanning horizontally or vertically. It produces a symmetrical beam 1 degree wide. The scopes may be used for either PPI or RHI presentation. The output power is 250 kilowatts, and the minimum signal which can be received is 10^{-13} watt. This equipment is very sensitive and sometimes can detect very light rainfall at ranges of over 100 miles.

The newest weather radar set is called the WSR-57. It is a 10-cm set designed by the U. S. Weather Bureau. One of the major reasons for choosing this wave length was that the major function of the radar is the detection of severe storms such as thunderstorms, tornadoes, and hurricanes, rather than clouds or light rain. As will be seen in the next chapter, radar sets operating at the longer wave lengths detect only the larger rain particles, but they can "see" through widespread cloud and rain systems. In order to obtain a narrow beam it was necessary to use a large antenna. Plate III shows a photograph of the antenna system. The circular dish is 3.7 meters in diameter. When the transmitter is operating, the antenna radiates 500 kilowatts of power. The receiver is capable of detecting signals as small as 10^{-14} watt.

As the reader can well imagine, there are many

other radar sets being employed by meteorologists. Surplus military equipment is still in widespread use. Other equipment specifically intended for weather observations has been produced by a number of companies in the United States, England, and Italy.

CHAPTER 3

RADAR DETECTS A RAINDROP

It is easy to visualize how a radar set detects an airplane if you will consider how the large searchlights used in the last war spotted bombers flying over London. A narrow but intense beam of light, when it was intercepted by an airplane, illuminated the airplane sufficiently for it to be seen from the ground. When we say it could be seen, we mean that the amount of light reflected was enough to register a visible image in the human eye.

If one were using a radar set, an electromagnetic wave having a wave length much longer than that of light would be transmitted in a narrow beam, and some of the beam would be reflected back. With a searchlight beam, there would be a continuous stream of outgoing and reflected energy. In this circumstance we learn only the direction to the airplane but not the range. With a radar set, which sends out a short burst of power and measures the time for the reflected pulse to return, both direction and range may be obtained.

Whether one used radar waves or light rays would

make little difference if one were concerned with mathematical calculations of the outgoing power that would be reflected from a large airplane. This is true because in both cases the wave lengths of the waves are very small in comparison with the dimensions of the target. The wave lengths of light and radar waves are in the vicinity of 0.5×10^{-4} cm and 10 cm, respectively, while a bombing airplane may be of the order of 3×10^3 cm long. As long as the target size greatly exceeds the wave length, one can use geometrical laws applying to light waves to calculate the amount of reflected radar energy.

When the target is small relative to the wave length or about the same as the wave length, the problem becomes more complicated. This is the condition when radar looks at a raindrop or a group of raindrops.

Reflection from a Single Small Raindrop

Consider first a single raindrop assumed to be spherical and having a diameter of 0.1 cm. It would be 100 times smaller than the wave length of a 10-cm radar set. How much power would the single particle send back to the radar antenna?

The solution to this problem was offered in 1871 by the famous English scientist Lord Rayleigh. At that time he obviously was not concerned with radar, an instrument developed some sixty years later. He was interested in the blue color of the sky.

It is well known that the visible light from the sun

is composed of all the colors in the spectrum from
violet to red.* This is clearly shown by the beautiful
rainbows you sometimes see in a summer shower.
Each of the colors represents an electromagnetic
wave having its own distinctive wave length. The
lengths of the waves increase as the color goes from
violet to blue to yellow to red. Lord Rayleigh showed
that air molecules and tiny dust particles scatter the
light striking them. He demonstrated that the shorter
wave lengths are scattered more readily than the long
ones. Thus, the violet and blue components of sun-
light are scattered downward much more than the
yellows and reds. Violet light has only a weak intensity, and as a result the sky is mostly blue. Lord Rayleigh developed an equation that applies when the
scattering particles are much smaller than the wave
length, and it is known that when raindrops are much
smaller than a radar wave length, they also follow
Rayleigh's scattering law.

In earlier paragraphs we used the term *reflection*
when referring to power returned to the radar receiver, but now the term *scatter* has been introduced.
In order to avoid confusion it is necessary to examine
how a spherical water drop behaves when it inter-
cepts a radar wave. As the wave passes over the drop,
a certain quantity of power is extracted. The water absorbs some of the wave energy and heats up by a very
slight amount. The remainder of the power is immediately re-radiated by the drop. Some of the re-

* See *Michelson and the Speed of Light* by Bernard Jaffe,
Science Study Series, S 13, for a detailed discussion of the
properties of light.

radiated power goes in all directions, but the amounts radiated outward from the radar set and back toward the radar set exceed the amounts radiated in a direction perpendicular to the beam. The behavior of the drop in radiating the intercepted power is referred to as scattering. The power which is scattered directly back toward the radar is called *back-scattered power*, and it is this power alone which can be considered to be reflected back by the drop.

With large targets the amount of outgoing power that is reflected back is proportional to the cross-sectional area of the target. The Rayleigh scattering law shows that this is certainly not the case with very small targets, such as clouds or raindrops. According to this law, if the wave length remains fixed, the back-scattered power is proportional to the sixth power of the drop diameter. As an example, consider a 10-cm radar set. If the back-scattered power of a drop of diameter 0.1 cm were P, then that from a 0.2 cm drop would be $2 \times 2 \times 2 \times 2 \times 2 \times 2 \times P$ or 64P, and the power from a 0.3 cm drop would be 729P. If the reflected power depended only on the cross-sectional areas, then the values corresponding to drops of diameters 0.1, 0.2, and 0.3 cm would be P, 4P, and 9P respectively. Quite evidently the amount of power back-scattered by a drop is greatly dependent on the diameter of the drop.

Rayleigh's law also tells us something about the effects of wave length. It states that back-scattering is inversely proportional to the fourth power of the wave length. Therefore, if the drop diameter is fixed, the reflection would be considerably higher if a short wave length were used. For example, the back-scattering of 5-cm radio waves would be 16 times greater than that of 10-cm waves, if all other factors remained unchanged. Thus, it can be concluded that if you wish to obtain strong echoes from very small drops, you should use a radar set operating at a very short wave length.

When one makes a decision as to the best wave length to use for observing raindrops, several other factors besides radar reflectivity must be considered. One of the most important, called *attenuation*, is the weakening of the outgoing and reflected wave by intervening clouds and raindrops. It has been found that the shorter the wave length, the stronger the attenuation. For this reason, when rainstorms covering large regions are to be observed, radar sets operating at longer wave lengths (10 to 20 cm) are better because the weakenings of the signal by absorption and scattering are very small in comparison to the effects at the shorter wave lengths (1 to 3 cm).

It can be seen that when one selects a radar set for the detection of raindrops, two conflicting factors must be resolved. It is desirable to have a short wave length in order to be able to detect very small drops, but it is desirable to have a long wave length in order to reduce attenuation effects. Obviously it is necessary to compromise. A number of experts have suggested that a 5-cm radar set is ideal. In practice, wave lengths of about 1, 3, 5, 10, and 20 cm have been used for various purposes. Providing the advantages and disadvantages are recognized, each one can adequately perform certain observation jobs.

Up to this point only raindrops have been mentioned. What is the effect on the radar reflectivity if the drop suddenly freezes? When only small particles are involved, the result is simply a reduction of the echo intensity by about 5 times. What happens to radar echoes from large ice particles we shall see in the next chapter.

Back-scattering by a Group of Raindrops

One can easily calculate the power back-scattered to a radar set from a single raindrop; it is too small to be detected by ordinary radar receivers. For example, a raindrop of diameter 0.1 cm at a range of 10 kilometers would back-scatter about 6×10^{-20} watt to a 10-cm radar of the type used for weather observations. This value is much smaller than the 10^{-13} watt that is the minimum detectable signal of many radar sets.

Of course, raindrops never occur in so few numbers that only one will appear in the radar beam at the same time. Observations have shown, in general, that the number of raindrops per unit volume decreases with increasing drop diameter and that the actual numbers vary widely. Most often the number of raindrops per cubic meter of air is between 100 and 1000.

Consider a radar set with a symmetrical beam having a width of 3 degrees and a pulse length of 300 meters. All the raindrops within a volume (Fig. 8) enclosed by the beam and a distance equal to one-half the pulse length can reflect power back to the radar set so that the reflections arrive at the *same instant*. The explanation of why only half the pulse length is used to define the volume is complicated, and, since this point is not particularly important to this discussion, it will not be pursued. It would serve as a good problem to an interested reader to prove to himself that the statement about the pertinent volume is true.

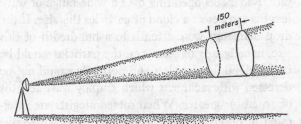

FIG. 8. *Power returned from all the drops in the unshaded part of the beam reaches the radar set at the same instant. The sides of this volume, a truncated cone, are the beam boundaries; its altitude is 150 m, half the pulse length.*

If at a range of 10 kilometers the radar beam were filled with raindrops in a concentration of $500/m^3$, the total number of drops back-scattering power to the radar would be given by the volume times the concentration. In the case of a typical weather radar with a 3-degree beam width and a 300-meter pulse length there would be about 2×10^{10} drops. And if the power back-scattered from a single drop were 6×10^{-20} watt, the average power received from the rainstorm would be 12×10^{-10} watt. In this situation an echo would certainly be seen on the radarscope. Note that the effects of attenuation have been neglected. This step can usually be taken safely as long as wave lengths equal to, or greater than, 10 cm are employed. When shorter wave lengths are used, appropriate corrections can be made.

A water drop with a diameter of 0.1 cm is large enough to be regarded as rain because such a drop can fall many thousands of feet before it will evaporate. Radar sets operating over a wide range of wave lengths can detect a cloud of particles this size. If the drop diameters were a tenth to a hundredth of this size, namely 0.01 or 0.001 cm, the particles would be in the cloud droplet class and normally would not be detected with radar sets which employ wave lengths of 10 cm or greater. When meteorologists are interested in observing clouds, they use radar with wave lengths in the vicinity of 1 cm.

In Chapter 5 we shall deal with the use of radar for measuring rainfall intensity and will return to the subject of the scattering of radar waves by raindrops. Before we go into these matters in more detail, however, it is important to look at the reflection from large particles in the atmosphere. Hailstones are the largest particles produced in clouds, and the next chapter will consider their reactions with radar waves.

CHAPTER 4

RADAR DETECTS A HAILSTONE

When it was discovered that radar could locate rainstorms, meteorologists quickly moved the device into the arsenal of weather observing equipment, and scientists began to look for other applications. Early in the game attempts were made to devise techniques for observing a form of precipitation which causes damage in the millions of dollars every year —hail.

Almost everyone, at one time or another, has seen hailstones. They are large particles of ice which fall out of some thunderstorms. In many parts of the world they appear only rarely, but in some areas they occur with discouraging regularity. Among the unlucky places are the western Great Plains of the United States and Canada, northern Italy, southern Germany, and the Caucasus region in the southern part of the Soviet Union. In these areas hailstorms not only occur frequently, but also with a violence that beats crops into the ground, strips fruit off trees, and causes widespread damage to buildings.

Hailstones exceeding three inches in diameter have

been observed in various parts of the world. In eastern Colorado, a favorite hunting ground of hailstorms, about one of every seven storms contains some stone exceeding one inch in diameter. Plate IV shows a photograph of a large stone which fell in this region.

Hail not only menaces people and things on the ground but also represents a hazard to airplanes. The hazard grows as airplane speeds increase. A jet airplane which encounters a two-inch hailstone while flying at 500 mph can suffer serious damage. The U. S. Air Force has reported that one of its jet bombers was forced to land, critically damaged, after it flew into hail exceeding two inches in diameter at an altitude of 30,000 feet. At one time it was felt that at such high altitudes the hail danger would be slight, but now that we actually are flying there, we find that the stones are carried up by the updrafts in the thunderstorms.

It is clear that it would be very valuable to be able to examine a thunderstorm with a radar set and find out whether or not it had hail and to observe how large the stones were. Unfortunately, hail usually occurs together with rain, and the hail echo on a PPI radarscope is similar in many respects to the echo from a thundershower in which only rain is present. See Plate V.

In 1955 Henry T. Harrison, director of meteorology at United Air Lines, and his group did some research on reflections from hailstorms and concluded that echoes having particular types of shapes and particular intensities were likely to indicate hail. On the basis of this work they instructed their pilots to avoid such echoes by a distance of five miles or more. With an airborne radarscope in the cockpit, the pilot could easily follow this rule. Since the procedure was adopted in about 1956, United Air Lines planes in flight have suffered no significant hail damage.

Although the technique of avoiding suspicious thunderstorm echoes has worked well, scientists still are concerned with learning how to employ radar to discriminate between hail and rain and how to estimate the sizes of the stones. During the last few years great strides have been made in this direction.

An important step was taken in 1957 when Ralph J. Donaldson made careful observations of the intensities of the echoes from hail-producing thunderstorms. He found that the intensities were much greater than one would expect with even excessive amounts of rain. Similar types of observations were made shortly thereafter in England. David Atlas, a colleague of Donaldson at the U. S. Air Force Cambridge Research Center, working with Frank H. Ludlam of the Imperial College of London, suspected that the reason for the strong echoes was that hailstones were more reflective than the water drops. It appears offhand that this was an assumption which should have been made and tested long ago. As a matter of fact, in 1946 J. W. Ryde in England published an article in which he had calculated that hailstones had high radar reflectivities, but the results were not generally recognized. Many workers in the field were misled by the fact that when very small sizes are involved, ice particles have about five times less reflectivity than do water particles.

At any rate, in 1959 Atlas, Ludlam, and his co-workers set out to measure the back-scattering of hailstones. Their experiment was simple in design but yielded the information they sought. First they made spherical ice balls by freezing water in molds. Then they suspended the ice spheres in a nylon net about

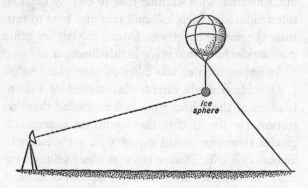

FIG. 9. *Experimental procedure for measuring the radar-reflecting properties of ice spheres.*

150 feet below a tethered balloon located about one mile from their radar set. See Fig. 9. The temperature of the ice spheres had been lowered to below −40°C in a deep-freeze box. Because of their temperature the spheres stayed dry at an altitude of several hundred feet long enough for a series of measurements to be taken. Melting did not start until the outer layer of ice warmed to 0°C. Observations were continued over periods of time to allow the ice

spheres to begin to melt, so that the effects of a water coat could be determined.

The Mie Theory

After learning about the preliminary results at Imperial College, the author and Benjamin M. Herman began theoretical calculations of the back-scattering from dry and wet ice spheres at The University of Arizona. An electronic computer, which could handle in a short time the complicated theory applying to these problems, did the job. The theory was first proposed by Gustav Mie in 1908 and has been applied to a wide variety of problems where electromagnetic waves are scattered by spherical particles. This is the same theory that Ryde used in 1946 to investigate dry hailstones. Experimental and theoretical work concerned with these problems was independently being carried on at the University of Texas under John R. Gerhardt.

When the theoretical and experimental results were compared, they were found to be in close agreement. The combined efforts of scientists on two sides of the Atlantic demonstrated that a single large hailstone was capable of scattering back to a radar set many millions of times more power than a single raindrop. It became evident that the intense echoes observed by Donaldson were caused by the hailstones within the thunderstorm.

The research also showed that when an ice sphere

develops a thin coat of water it scatters radar waves as if it consisted entirely of water. A large hailstone is capable of producing a strong signal because ice absorbs radar waves poorly and allows the stone to behave as a lens. The incoming power is focused on the back side of a sphere and then reflected backward toward the radar. When the ice begins to melt, the

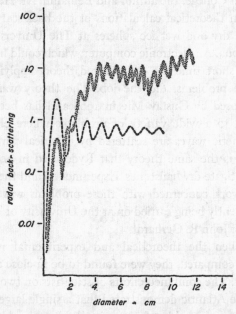

FIG. 10. *Relative back-scattering properties of water and ice spheres when a 3-cm radar set is employed. The dashed line is for water, the other for ice. The vertical scale is actually a function called the "normalized back-scattering cross-section." The returned power is proportional to the number on the vertical scale multiplied by the area of the sphere involved.*

conditions change rapidly. Water absorbs the radar energy much more strongly than does ice. As a result, when a water film only 0.01 cm thick covers the stone, most of the intercepted energy is absorbed before focusing can occur, and there is scattering from the convex front edge of the sphere. The net effect is a reduction of the power back-scattered to the radar set.

The relative amounts of power received by a 3-cm radar set from water and ice spheres of various sizes are shown in Fig. 10. As was noted in Chapter 3, when very small particles are involved, water back-scatters better than ice. For large particles, the reverse is true. When a thin layer of water, about 0.1 mm thick, forms on ice particles, the water curve approximately describes the echoing characteristics of the particles.

Echo Intensity

The application of the Mie theory and the experimental results clearly demonstrated that when scattering particles have diameters close to, or greater than, the wave length of the radar set, the simple Rayleigh Law discussed in the preceding chapter is no longer applicable. The back-scattering property of a large particle cannot be written out as a simple equation with several terms but, rather, takes a complicated mathematical form which leads to the many oscillations of the curves shown in Fig. 10.

It has become clear that in some cases, it is possible on the basis of the echo intensity alone to infer whether or not hail is present. When the echo intensity exceeds the amount which one would reasonably expect to obtain from maximum rates of rainfall, it can be assumed that hailstones are present.

Another piece of echo information can be used when one is trying to determine whether or not a thunderstorm contains hail. First Donaldson, and then Richard H. Douglas at McGill University, showed that the greater the vertical extent of a thunderstorm, the higher the probability of hail. This relationship appears to be founded on the need for strong updrafts in thunderstorms that produce hail. If a hailstone is to grow to a diameter of several centimeters, it must remain in the upper part of the thundercloud for ten to twenty minutes. In order for this to occur there must be strong updrafts which can lift the stone.

One may conclude that thunderstorms extending to very great altitudes, into the base of the stratosphere for example, and having very intense echoes will contain hail. Also, the higher the echo intensity the larger will be the stones.

The information gained from the theoretical calculations and experimental studies of the back-scattering properties of hail has led Atlas and Ludlam to propose a technique allowing estimates of the size of the hailstones as well as the number per unit volume in the cloud. It involves measurements of echo intensity with three radar sets operating at different wave lengths. For each wave length there is a curve somewhat similar to the ice curve of Fig. 10

but with the peaks and troughs displaced to the right or left. By matching the power measurements with the set of three curves, it should be possible to find which hailstone sizes could reasonably be expected to be present. This new procedure is being tested at the present time.

It now appears that the hailstones which usually conceal themselves in a cover of raindrops can be ferreted out with radar.

CHAPTER 5

MEASURING RAINFALL
WITH RADAR

Because of the importance of water in almost all aspects of human activity, people have been measuring and keeping records of rainfall for a long, long time. Fortunately, if someone is interested in knowing how much rain falls at a particular point, this information is easy to get. An ordinary bucket can serve as a rain gauge, provided it is set away from trees and buildings and account is taken of the taper of the sides of the bucket. As a matter of fact, most rainfall records in the archives of the weather observers around the world have been obtained with what might be considered glorified buckets.

The standard U. S. Weather Bureau rain gauge, as shown in Fig. 11, consists of a cylindrical vessel with an opening 8 inches in diameter. The captured rain water is funneled into a narrow inner cylinder. The amount of rain may be measured by dipping a stick in the water and reading a level mark, as you would check the oil in your car. The narrow cylinder has a cross-sectional area one-tenth the area of the opening through which the rain falls. When a stick dipped into the narrow cylinder shows that the depth of the water is 2.0 inches, we can easily calculate that 0.2 inch of rain fell. To make reading of the rainfall quick and easy, the stick is marked in units giving rainfall directly.

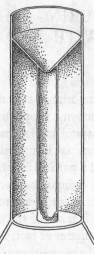

FIG. 11. *Standard U. S. Weather Bureau rain gauge.*

Other countries have gauges similar in principle to the U.S. gauge, but they differ in detail. For example, the area of the gauge openings differ. All the gauges serve merely to collect water.

When the precipitation is in the form of snow, the amount given in the records corresponds to the depth of water after the snow is melted. As a rough rule of thumb, you can figure that a depth of snow of 10 inches corresponds to about 1 inch of water.

The stick gauge yields information only when

enough water has accumulated to be read off the stick; in other words, over a fairly long period of time. This scheme is generally used only when the measurements are to be made at intervals of several hours. As a result, it tells us little about the rainfall rate, that is, the rainfall per minute or per hour. When meteorologists want rate information, more complicated gauges are employed. These gauges still use the same type of opening to catch the precipitation but the way of reading the quantity is different. Two of the most widely used are known as the *tipping bucket* and the *weighing gauge*.

In the tipping bucket gauge the water collected is fed by a funnel to a narrow opening through which the water falls into one of two small buckets at the end of a rocking arm. The bucket holds an amount of water equivalent to 0.01 inch of rain. The mounting is such that when the bucket is filled, it suddenly tips over and empties the water. When this occurs, the rain water begins to fill the second bucket. When the second is filled, it suddenly tips and empties, and the first one returns to its original position ready to be filled again. The times when the small buckets tip are noted on a recorder. Since the quantity of water needed to fill the bucket is known, the rate of rainfall is obtained by counting the number of times the bucket has tipped over during any interval of time, for example one hour.

As the name implies, the weighing gauge employs a scale to weigh the rain. The precipitation falling through the upper opening of the gauge falls into a pail sitting on a scale. The movement of the scale is recorded on a moving strip of paper. As water or snow accumulates in the pail, the pen arm moves progressively up the recorder chart, which is turned by a clock mechanism. Since the weight per unit volume of water is known, the weight of the total quantity of collected water can be interpreted in terms of depth of rainfall. By noting the rate at which the trace on the chart rises with the passage of time, one can calculate the precipitation rate.

If one is concerned with the total rainfall at a particular point, any of these three schemes will give satisfactory measurements, but it must be clearly recognized that they give information applying strictly to only a very small area. To be specific, it applies only to the area of the opening of the gauge. In winter storms the variations over small distances sometimes are small, and a measurement at a single point may be representative of the rainfall within some miles of the gauge. But during periods of summer showers and thunderstorms the variations of rainfall over small distances can be very great. The diameters of showers may be as small as 2 or 3 miles, with sharp boundaries between areas of rain and those of no rain. It is not unusual to have heavy rain on one side of town and none on the other. In this circumstance a single rain gauge in the center of town would represent a very small area. Since it is not practical to have a rain gauge every mile or two all over the country, we have been forced to be satisfied with unrepresentative rainfall records. With the introduction of radar, however, it has become possible to make a drastic change in this situation.

Radar Measurements of Precipitation Rate

In Chapter 3 it was shown that the power received from a cloud of raindrops was related to the size of the drops. If one knows the characteristics of the radar set accurately, one can write an equation

$$P = \frac{A \times N \times D^6}{r^2} \qquad (1)$$

where P is the average power back-scattered from a region of raindrops of average diameter D* located at a range r. The quantity A is a constant factor that depends mostly on the properties of the radar set. N is the number of drops per unit volume. This equation applies as long as the wave length of the radar set is much greater than the diameter of the raindrops. If we use a 10-cm radar set, it will apply to all rains since raindrops seldom exceed a diameter of about 0.8 cm.

If it could be shown that a relationship existed between the term $(N \times D^6)$ and the rainfall intensity, R, this equation could be rewritten with P in terms of R. If all the drops were the same size, this could be done easily. Unfortunately, this is almost never the case. Large drops are less numerous than small drops. Fig. 12 shows how the number varies with size in one rain. Many measurements show that the curve of

* To be exact, the correct average diameter D is obtained by computing D^6 for each drop, getting the sum, dividing by the number of drops, and taking the one-sixth power of the result.

number versus size changes from one rain to the next, and that the changes are particularly great from one *type* of rain to another. For example, the rains that fall on the mountains of tropical islands differ a great deal from the rains of thunderstorms over large continents. These variations make the problem of relating D to R more difficult but not impossible.

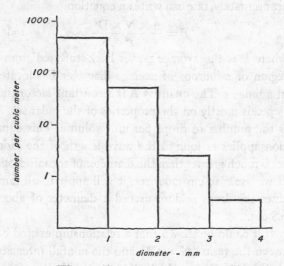

FIG. 12. *The number of rain drops per cubic meter in various size intervals in a typical rain shower.*

In various parts of the world measurements have been made of the diameters of raindrops and of the rainfall rate. Statistical studies have yielded various relations between D and R. It has been concluded that for most rains, except certain tropical rains and drizzle, one can obtain satisfactory results with the following equation:

$$N \times D^6 = 200 \times R^{1.6} \qquad (2)$$

After substituting in the earlier equation we get

$$P = \frac{C \times R^{1.6}}{r^2} \qquad (3)$$

where C is a constant given by the product $200 \times A$. We now have an equation that permits us to calculate the rainfall intensity R if we know the range of the storm, r, and the returned power, P. These two pieces of information can be obtained directly from the radar set. In the case of snow one can derive a similar type of equation.

Tests of equation (3) have been made by carefully measuring the rainfall over a fixed area at a known range while simultaneously measuring the power back-scattered to the radar from a volume of drops just above the area. If the radar measurements are to have meaning in this experiment, the radar beam must be as close to the ground as possible. Then the raindrops observed by the radar are close to the same size as those falling into the rain gauges. If the beam is pointed too high, the readings may not give a true picture because the raindrops can either grow by collision or, in some cases, break up before they reach the ground.

Pauline M. Austin and her colleagues at the Massachusetts Institute of Technology have done some outstanding work in comparing radar observations of rainfall with rain gauge measurements. They took great care in all aspects of the work, using special gauges, which would give accurate readings of rainfall rate, and a special technique for measuring the received back-scattered power.

The quantity P given in equation (3) refers to the average power returned from the raindrops over the gauges. Raindrops are in constant movement because of the effects of gravity and of the turbulent movement of the air. As a result, P varies rapidly from instant to instant. On an A-scope, a rain echo looks something like a field of tall grass oscillating up and down. By watching the scope, one can note the level around which the signals oscillate, and in this way arrive at a good estimate of the average power.

A better way to measure P is to use a device called a *pulse integrator*. This instrument adds up the signal voltage from a large number of pulses and computes the average voltage. Knowing this quantity, one may obtain P because it is approximately equal to the square of the average signal voltage. This is the technique employed by Dr. Austin in her research.

The investigations at M.I.T. and various other institutions have showed that a carefully calibrated radar, operating at wave lengths subject to little attenuation, yielded values of precipitation rates that were consistently too low by a small amount. A satisfactory reason for the difference has not yet been found. But since it is consistently in one direction, one can take this difference into account by multiplying the right side of equation (3) by an appropriate factor. With a 10-cm radar set 0.2 appears to be a proper figure. When this correction has been made, rainfall rate can be measured with satisfactory accuracy.

Measurement of Rainfall over a Small Area

Hydrologists and meteorologists who deal with river flows are not primarily concerned with the rainfall rates at a point. Instead, they want to know how much rain has fallen over a watershed in the last hour, or last few hours. With this information they can make calculations of the rate at which the water will flow into the streams and creeks and later into the rivers. Thus they can predict the levels of water in the various channels and make flood forecasts. Knowing how much rain fell, where and when, water engineers may be able to avert floods by releasing water from dams in order that new water coming downstream can be captured and released in controlled quantities.

Over most watersheds there are networks of rain gauges spaced some tens of miles apart. The measurements from these gauges are used for *isohyetal maps*, maps showing lines of equal rainfall. In order to draw such maps accurately one must have sufficient experience to make educated guesses on the location of the lines. On the map given in Fig. 13, the line corresponding to 0.5 inch of rain could be shifted by a substantial amount. When one station has 1.0 inch and another station 20 miles away has no rain, the location of the 0.5 line could go almost anywhere in between. This vagueness is a problem in mapping the rainfall from thunderstorms; the possibilities of errors are great. When the rain is more or less steady over a large region, drawing isohyets becomes easier because there is less variation over small distances. An experienced analyst who has spent many years working with rainfall data and is familiar with the characteristics of different cloud systems usually can arrive at an analysis close to the correct one. But on occasions when isolated thunderstorms produce intense rainfall even the experts can produce an isohyetal map that is seriously in error.

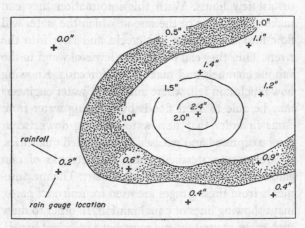

FIG. 13. *An isohyetal map. Each cross marks the location of a rain gauge; the number plotted above it gives the amount of rainfall in inches. The heavy lines represent lines of equal rainfall, or isohyets.*

Once a flood forecaster has drawn the isohyets, he can make estimates of the total rainfall by measuring the areas between isohyets and multiplying them by the average rainfall over that area. For example, if the shaded area in Fig. 13 is measured to be 22 square miles, you would multiply by the average rainfall, namely 0.75 inch of rain. In this case it would be found that the total rainfall amounts to about 38 million cubic feet of water. By repeating this procedure for each area between isohyets and adding the products, you would obtain the total quantity of rain water.

It is clear that if the isohyets are not positioned correctly, the total rain water calculated by this procedure will be in error. Radar can observe the rain patterns and can give some information as to the lateral extent of the precipitation. This additional information is of assistance in drawing the isohyets. In this role radar serves merely to assist the analyst by supplying another piece of information which is used along with the rain gauge observations. Radar can be used in a more direct way.

In 1948 Horace R. Byers proposed that a radar set could be made to yield the total precipitation over a small area if it were properly calibrated for this purpose. His scheme involved measuring the echo area at 5-minute intervals, computing the average, and then multiplying by the duration of the storm. The quantity so obtained was compared graphically with the actual total rain that fell on a test area in which rain gauges were spaced at one-mile intervals. It was possible to draw a "calibration curve" relating echo area to total rainfall. Once such a curve was obtained, it was possible, from measurements of the echo area, to estimate the total rainfall. This scheme was almost strictly statistical in nature. Echo intensity was not taken into account.

A more refined procedure proposed by Vaugh

Rockney of the U. S. Weather Bureau and investigated thoroughly by Homer W. Hiser and his associates at the University of Miami, photographically accomplishes the echo-area averaging and at the same time takes into account the echo intensity. After the radar set is carefully adjusted, a camera on the PPI is used to take a long time exposure of the scope picture. If one wishes to know the rainfall over a particular area for the period 12:00 noon to 3:00 P.M., a continuous exposure is made for that period. With a radar set having an antenna rotating ten times per minute, this would result in a multiple exposure of 1800 separate scope pictures. As echoes move across the scope, their images appear on the photograph as smeared echoes. The intensity of the echo at any point on the film depends on two factors: (1) the intensity of the echo and (2) the duration of the echo. To use this technique one must have special film and carry out careful film processing.

Once the film negative has been obtained, the intensity of the echo images are measured by means of a device known as a *photo densitometer*. It measures the intensity of the echoes by measuring how much light passes through the film. The film density is obtained at locations where rain gauges exist, and this information is used with the radar range to plot curves showing the rain intensity. Fig. 14 shows a graph obtained by this procedure. On the horizontal axis is plotted the film density, while on the vertical is range. At each point on the graph paper corresponding to a rain gauge, you plot the rain measured by the gauge during the period of interest, for example,

12:00 noon to 3:00 P.M. If sufficient gauges are scattered in the area, it becomes possible to draw lines of constant rainfall. Each line tells what combinations of range and film density correspond to rainfall shown plotted on the line. This diagram may be regarded as a calibration chart for the radar set and the film. Once a diagram such as this one has been obtained, it is possible to go back to the film and measure the rainfall at places where there are no gauges. This in-

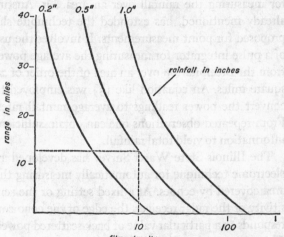

FIG. 14. *Curves show amounts of rainfall plotted as functions of the intensity of the echoes on long time-exposure film and related to the range from observation point to the point of interest. For example, if the film density were 10 at a range of 14 miles, the amount of rainfall at that point should be 0.5 inches.* (From a report by M. H. Hiser and associates at the University of Miami.)

volves measuring the range to the place, measuring the film density, and then going to the diagram to see where the horizontal and vertical lines corresponding to these figures intersect.

One may use this procedure to calculate the rainfall at enough points to obtain accurate isohyetal maps of total rainfall. This procedure, in turn, should lead to accurate estimates of the total rainfall over a watershed.

Several electronic schemes have been developed for measuring the rainfall over an area. Dr. Austin, already mentioned, has extended the technique she proposed for point measurements. It involves the use of a pulse integrator for measuring the average power from the precipitation over an area of the order of 20 square miles. An equation like (3) was employed to convert the power readings to average rainfall rates. From repeated observations one can obtain sufficient information to yield total rainfall.

The Illinois State Water Survey has developed an electronic technique for automatically measuring the area covered by echoes. At a fixed setting of the sensitivity of the radar receiver, the edge of the echo corresponds to a particular value of back-scattered power. This quantity is related to a value of rainfall rate which can be calculated from equation (3). By varying the sensitivity of the radar receiver in a stepwise fashion, the areal extent of various rates of precipitation can be observed. The device is designed to yield a single number which, when multiplied by an appropriate constant, yields the average rainfall over an entire watershed.

The advantages of the electronic scheme for measuring total precipitation are that, at least in principle, little manual labor is needed to obtain the important piece of information—namely, how much rain fell. On the other hand, the operation is complicated, not entirely reliable at this time, and of course expensive. The long-exposure film technique is fairly simple and appears to be reliable.

It should be noted that all the procedures discussed require that the antenna beam be close to the ground. This requirement makes it very difficult to use radar for rainfall measurements in mountainous regions because only a small fraction of a drainage area can be covered at one time. Over flat or rolling terrain the procedures are useful.

The application of radar techniques for rainfall measurement have lagged behind the development of the device itself. In some cases radar data have been used to assist in drawing isohyetal maps, but little use has been made of the more refined techniques. However, at the present time (1961) there is a strong impetus in the direction of making fuller use of radar, and it appears that in the near future radar will become an important instrument for observing rainfall over watersheds.

CHAPTER 6

THE FORMATION OF
RAIN AND SNOW

When they hear the term "natural resource," most people probably think of minerals which come out of the ground. In recent years scientists have become more concerned with the resources of the atmosphere, rain and snow. From all parts of the world there come reports of water shortages. This situation is particularly severe in the arid and semiarid regions but is not restricted to these places. As the world's population booms to ever increasing numbers, as farmers begin to make more extensive use of irrigation, and as industry continues to expand in all parts of the globe, the needs for fresh water will certainly become greater and greater. In some regions the shortage of inexpensive water may be the limiting factor in economic growth.

At the present time there are only two major sources of fresh water: (1) the large stored supplies of water in lakes and in the underground basins and (2) rain and snow. Great efforts are being devoted to the development of techniques for desalting ocean water, but up to the present year (1961) the water produced in this way is still far too expensive for agricultural and industrial purposes.

The supplies of water in lakes are of great value to the communities near them but sometimes are of relatively little value to areas several hundred miles away. The laying of pipes and installation and operation of pumps make transportation costs too high. It may be surprising, but it is true, that during prolonged hot weather with little rain, some of the suburbs of Chicago have had serious water shortages even though they are less than fifty miles from one of the largest fresh water lakes in the world—Lake Michigan.

In some regions, southern Arizona for example, most of the water used for irrigation and municipal purposes is pumped from the underground reservoirs. Unfortunately, the rate at which this water is being replenished by seepage of rain water is almost insignificant. The water being pumped is very old. It was left there back in the ice age. The supply of this so-called connate water is limited. As long as the pumps operate, the water level keeps dropping. The total amount of water underground is quite large, no doubt, but the deeper you have to go, the more expensive it becomes. Other sources of water must be tapped in areas such as this one.

One source that needs exploitation is the atmosphere. As the winds blow over the earth, they pick up, as a result of evaporation from the oceans and the continents, huge quantities of water vapor. It has been truly stated that the "atmosphere is an ocean of low density water." If one could take a column of air extending from the earth's surface to an altitude of about 30,000 feet and squeeze out all the water vapor, the water would amount to a depth ranging from a few tenths of an inch to as much as perhaps two inches. The lowest amounts would be found in cold dry regions; the highest in warm moist ones. For example, in southern Arizona in July and August the total water depth averages more than an inch. This may not seem like much water, but if one inch is multiplied by the total number of square inches of land in the state of Arizona, one obtains a quantity of water which is impressive indeed. Also, it should be noted that as the winds blow over the state there is a constant inflow of water-bearing air.

A vital question is, How much of the water vapor over a region actually falls as rain or snow? Meteorologists sometimes phrase the question differently. They ask, How efficient are the rain producing processes? In other words, of the water that exists over an area in the form of vapor, what per cent actually reaches the ground? The efficiency, defined in this way, varies greatly from one part of the world to the next.

In cold, wet areas such as the islands in the Alaskan chain, the efficiency is close to 100 per cent. On the other hand, in arid regions such as Arizona the efficiency during the summer rainy season is only about 5 per cent. If one could increase the efficiency by only a small amount, let us say to 6 per cent, the rainfall would be increased by 20 per cent. Unfortunately, we do not know how to accomplish this feat. This is the problem scientists all over the world have been trying to solve for many years—namely, weather modification. Modern attempts to stimulate rainfall date back to 1946 when Irving Langmuir and Vincent J. Schaefer showed that it was possible to modify certain types of clouds by sowing them with dry ice pellets. Since that time some progress has been made in developing techniques for modifying clouds, but there is still no basis for statements that rainfall can be increased from any cloud system or in any region of the world.

The major reason why meteorologists still are unable to change the weather is a lack of understanding of the ways by which nature produces rain. The fact of the matter is that we still are not sure how nature does it in all cases.

Summer Showers and Thunderstorms

Not too many years ago it was felt that virtually all precipitation was formed as frozen particles. When the air near the ground was warm, the ice crystals or snowflakes forming high in the atmosphere melted to become rain. The basis for this generalization was some excellent work published in the early thirties by Tor Bergeron. We now believe that the process he proposed does account for much of the precipitation reaching the earth's surface, but we have learned also that at least one more process is very important. This second process, known as the *coalescence process*, involves the growth of raindrops by the collision and merging of smaller cloud particles. For rain to form in this way, ice crystals are not necessary, but nature must produce some large cloud droplets which fall faster than the rest and cause many collisions.

Radar played an important role in proving that the coalescence process is effective in convective clouds, those billowing cauliflower clouds which sometimes grow into thunderstorms. With vertically scanning radar sets it was possible to observe building clouds and note at what elevations the first precipitation drops appeared. The upward and downward spread of the region of large drops could then be followed by continuing to observe the same cloud. This procedure led to a collection of observations such as the one series shown in Plate VI. It is made of eleven different radar observations taken at intervals of about 10 to 80 seconds. The time of each observation in minutes and seconds is shown under each small panel. The bottom of the photograph is near the earth's surface; the top is just over 20,000 feet.

In the cloud corresponding to the radar echoes of Plate VI, the first echo extended to an altitude of about 10,000 feet where the temperature was 52°F (+10°C). The echo grew rapidly both upward and downward, but even when it attained maximum size, its top had just about reached the level of 32°F, which was at 16,500 ft. It is not reasonable to expect that the rain from this cloud could have been formed by the ice-crystal mechanism because the temperatures were too high.

A large number of radar observations such as this one have been obtained in various parts of the United States, Australia, and England, and it is now accepted that the coalescence process plays an important role in the formation of showers. It might be asked, "Why hadn't this been established before the introduction of radar?" One of the chief reasons is that without radar it is all but impossible to know when and where the large drops first appear. By the time the raindrops fall out of the cloud base, the cloud top may have grown many thousands of feet and be at a temperature of 5°F (−15°C) or colder where ice crystals could form readily. This result could lead to the false assertion that the ice crystals led to the precipitation.

At the present time we still do not know the relative importance of the two rain-producing mechanisms. As we learn more on this subject, it will become easier to plan cloud modification projects.

Some Properties of Convective Clouds

Radar observations have led to a better knowledge of convective clouds. From observations with various types of radar equipment, we have found that sometimes a single narrow echo tower will build to great altitudes. In some cases a cloud with an echo two or three miles in diameter will grow to an altitude of perhaps seven or eight miles. Most often, however, the great thunderstorms grow in a stepwise fashion. An echo tower will grow steadily to an altitude of perhaps 25,000 ft and then begin to descend. After a few minutes another echo tower alongside the first will burst upward and grow to perhaps 35,000 ft. The process can be repeated until the thunderstorm penetrates into the stratosphere.

Each of the echo turrets can be considered a building block of the thunderstorm. It might also be regarded as a unit cell. Horace R. Byers and Roscoe R. Braham, Jr., from a study of a mass of observations obtained with all types of weather instruments, postulated the existence of "thunderstorm cells." They proposed that each cell follows a definable life cycle, which is fairly short, and that a thunderstorm may be composed of one or more cells. On the other hand, a group of English scientists led by R. S. Scorer and Frank H. Ludlam have put forth a different theory of thunderstorm growth. They suggest that in each thunderstorm there are large "bubbles" of air which rise from the ground to upper levels of the cloud. Although the theories differ in many respects, they allow for the formation of thunderstorms in stepwise fashion.

It has been found that the average growth rates of the tops of echoes in convective clouds is somewhere in the vicinity of 10 to 20 mph (about 5 to 10 meters per second), and that in some thunderstorms it may be two or three times as high. It is clear from these observations why airplanes penetrating these clouds sometimes experience strong updrafts and severe turbulence.

The duration of a thunderstorm may be of the order of an hour or so, as anyone knows who has had to wait for rain to stop before going home from work or school. It is interesting to note, however, that the duration of the individual echo towers or cells is fairly short. Radar observations show that the average is about 23 minutes. Of course, in a large thunderstorm there may be many cells next to one another, and from the time the rain starts to the time it stops can be many times 23 minutes. During this period, which may be several hours, the rate of rainfall is not constant. Instead, the intensity will reach a peak, then decrease and then increase again. Each peak corresponds to the passage of another tower. Next time you are waiting for a heavy rain shower to subside, check your watch and note how long it takes before a minimum in rain intensity occurs.

Wintertime Precipitation

In the warm seasons of the year most precipitation falls from showers and thunderstorms. Fairly isolated clouds build to great elevations, produce rain, and deposit it in the form of spotty showers. In these clouds the process of coalescence is quite important. The individual clouds themselves are characterized by small cross-sectional areas, strong updrafts and downdrafts, and durations measured in terms of an hour.

Most precipitation that falls in the cold months of the year comes from a different breed of clouds. Instead of isolated short-lived towers, there are widespread cloud systems with durations measured in terms of days. Instead of being of the order of 10 m/sec, the vertical air motions are usually less than 1 m/sec and may be less than 10 cm/sec.

The clouds from which most of the precipitation

falls are called *nimbostratus clouds*, that is, layer-type clouds which produce rain. They take shape as a result of slow but prolonged upward motion in the large cyclones that form and move with the westerly currents in the middle latitudes. It has been common to refer to the rain from these cloud systems as "continuous rain." As a matter of fact, it is more uniform than the rain from convective clouds. Nevertheless, when you view these systems with a radar set, it becomes quite clear that within regions where uniform precipitation might be expected there are centers of heavy precipitation. These observations indicate regions where the upward motion exceeds the average values by substantial amounts.

An excellent view of the mechanisms of winter precipitation is given in Plate VII, which was obtained at McGill University, Canada. This illustration was obtained with a radar set whose antenna was fixed and pointing vertically upward. Instead of scanning through a weather system, the set recorded the weather system's passing overhead. The photograph was obtained by moving film across the face of a scope on which there was a vertical line whose brightness increased at the ranges (that is, altitudes) at which there were echoes. The final picture can be considered to be composed of many thousands of closely spaced vertical lines.

Various aspects of Plate VII are revealing insofar as the precipitation mechanisms are concerned. It can be seen that above 8000 ft there are sloping streamers which lead up to vertically arrayed bright tufts. The scientists at McGill University, led by J. Stewart

Marshall, postulated that the bright tufts were regions in which ice crystals were formed and that the sloping streamers were the trajectories of the falling precipitation particles.

If the winds increase at a constant rate with increasing altitude and the rate of fall of the particles stays constant, one can derive a simple equation describing the trajectory. Marshall used observations similar to the one shown in this photograph to calculate the fall speed of the particles. In one well-documented case he found an average speed of about 4 ft/sec and concluded that the particles were aggregates of snow crystals.

When one examines the bright echo band extending across the photograph at an altitude of about 6000 ft, it becomes more certain that the particles were frozen, at least for the most part. This band occurs just below the melting level of 32°F (0°C). It has been noted by many observers and has been studied in some detail. J. W. Ryde, mentioned in an earlier chapter, was the first to offer a satisfactory explanation. His ideas were proposed in 1946, and although they have been refined by others, have been found to be essentially correct.

Ryde was the first to point out that when the reflecting particles were smaller than the wave length, they would be about five times more reflective in the liquid than in the frozen state. He suggested that the sudden increase of echo intensity just below the 0°C level occurred because falling snow particles melted rapidly. After the particles melted, he suggested, they would rapidly collapse into nearly spherical water

PLATE I. The antenna system of the AN/TPS-10, a 3-cm radar set. *(Photograph by Illinois State Water Survey.)*

PLATE II. Antenna system of the AN/CPS-9, a 3-cm weather radar set. *(Courtesy of the manufacturer, the Raytheon Company.)*

PLATE III. Radome being lowered over the antenna system of the Storm Finder Radar, WSR-57, a 10-cm weather radar set. The radome is transparent to the radar waves and protects the antenna from rain, snow, and wind. *(Courtesy of the manufacturer, the Raytheon Company.)*

PLATE IV. Photograph of a hailstone almost 3 inches in diameter. *(Courtesy of Dr. R. Schleusener, Colorado State University.)*

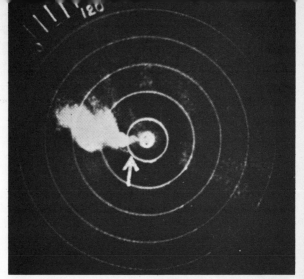

PLATE V. Thunderstorm with hail on PPI of a 5.5-cm airborne radar set. Range markers are at 5-mile intervals. The protruding echo to which the arrow points is interpreted as evidence of the presence of hail. *(Courtesy United Air Lines, Inc.)*

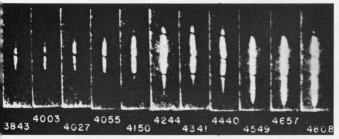

3843   4003   4027   4055   4150   4244   4341   4440   4549   4657   4808

PLATE VI. Growth of an echo in a shower cloud, observed with a vertically scanning 3-cm radar set. The top of the panel is just over 20,000 feet; the bottom is the earth's surface. Each panel represents a horizontal distance of about 14 miles. The numbers under each panel give the time of the observation in minutes and seconds.

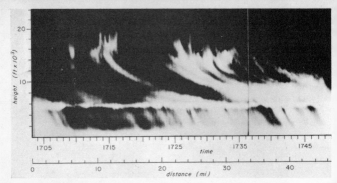

PLATE VII. Height-versus-time record of the echoes from a cloud system passing over Montreal, Canada. A vertically pointing 3-cm radar set was used to make these observations. The distance scale was calculated on the assumption that the weather pattern was moving at a speed of 63 mph, the wind speed at 18,000 feet. *(Courtesy Stormy Weather Group, McGill University.)*

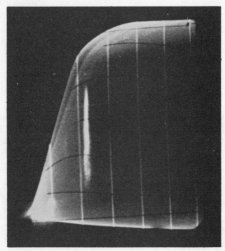

PLATE VIII. A thunderstorm echo at a range of 22 miles on the RHI of a 3-cm radar set. The dark, nearly horizontal lines are at intervals of 10,000 feet. The vertical lines are at intervals of 10 miles. Precipitation particles below about 12,000 feet cannot be seen as a radar echo because they are in the shadow of a mountain whose echo can be seen at a range of 10 miles.

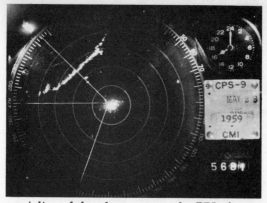

PLATE IX. A line of thunderstorms on the PPI of a 3-cm radar set. The heavy circular lines are at 50-mile intervals. *(Courtesy Illinois State Water Survey.)*

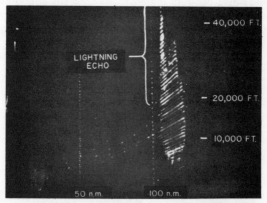

PLATE X. Echo from a lightning stroke on the RHI of a 10.7-cm radar set. This photograph was obtained by superimposing a negative transparency of the photograph of the radar-scope, when both the rain echo and lightning echo were present, and a positive transparency of a photograph of the scope showing only the rain echo just a short time earlier. Since the rain echo appears on both the negative and positive, the rain echoes tend to cancel each other while the lightning echo appears quite light. *(Courtesy Dr. D. Atlas, Air Force Cambridge Research Center.)*

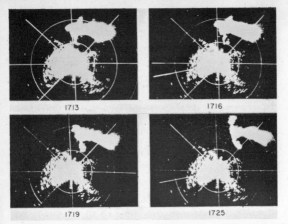

PLATE XI. Formation of a tornado "hook" can be followed on the scope of a 3-cm radar set in this sequence of radar observations. Reflections from the ground caused the large bright center and small dots. The tornado occurred in the most southerly portion of the finger protruding southward from the large thunderstorm echo. The time is shown in hours and minutes according to the 24-hour clock. *(From a paper by G. E. Stout and F. A. Huff, Bulletin American Meteorological Society, Vol. 34, 1953.)*

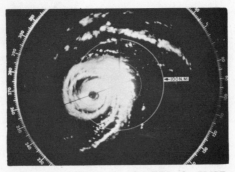

PLATE XII. Hurricane Donna on the PPI of a WSR-57 radar at the U. S. Weather Bureau, Miami, Florida. At the time the photograph was taken, 7:30 A.M. EST, September 10, 1960, the center of the hurricane was about 25 miles south of Everglades City. The circular markers are at 50-mile intervals *(Polaroid photo by L. F. Conover, National Hurricane Research Project.)*

PLATE XIII. Photographs of thunderstorm echoes observed with a 5.5-cm airborne radar set. The left-hand picture shows the normal PPI echoes; the photograph on the right shows the same echoes with isoecho contour circuitry turned on. The dark areas inside the echoes to the north and northeast show that these echoes are particularly intense. The range markers are at 5-mile intervals.

(Courtesy United Air Lines, Inc.)

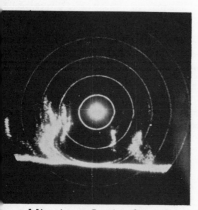

PLATE XIV. Shower and thunderstorm echoes on the scope of a vertically scannnig airborne 3-cm radar set. The coordinates of this picture are horizontal distance versus height. The circular lines are at 1-nautical mile (6076 feet) intervals. The nearly horizontal line is a reflection from the earth's surface. The position of the airplane is at the center of the picture. The thunderstorm echo to the left of center extends about 5000 feet above the flight altitude. The tops of the showers to the right of the center are about 6000 feet below flight altitude. This photograph was taken with the antenna scanning in the vertical plane perpendicular to the direction of flight. For use on commercial aircraft the antenna should scan in the vertical plane along the direction of flight.

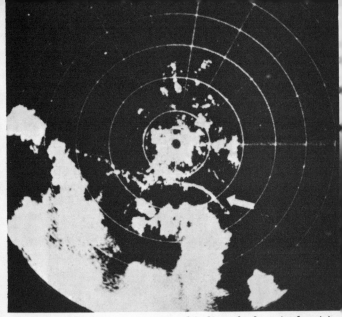

PLATE XVI. The arrow points to a thin line of echoes in the vicinity of a group of thunderstorms on the PPI of a 10-cm radar set. It has been established that lines such as these sometimes are caused by reflections from birds. The range markers are at 5-mile intervals. The white area and dots near the center of the scope are ground clutter. *(From a paper by W. G. Harper in the* Proceedings of Seventh Weather Radar Conference, *American Meteorological Society, 1958.*

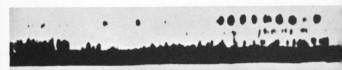

PLATE XV. The small series of dots seen on a vertically pointing 0.86-cm radar set are angel echoes. They are not reflections from airplanes or precipitation particles. The echoes are at an altitude of about 1000 to 2000 feet. Echoes appear dark against a white background because of photographic reversal. *(From a paper by R. B. Leasure, K. S. Durham, J. J. Tobias, and R. A. Dubrow.* Proceedings of Sixth Weather Radar Conference, *American Meteorological Society, 1957.)*

droplets which would fall more rapidly than snow-flakes. As a result, the drops would tend to move far-ther apart. The decrease in the number of drops in each unit volume of air would lead to fewer particles within the radar beam and a reduction of the echo intensity below the bright band. It can be seen that the echo streaks below the band are steeper than the echo streaks above it. This steepness shows that the particles are falling more rapidly in the region below the melting level.

On the basis of such observations as this it can be concluded that the rain falling from some winter storms originates at very low temperatures. In fairly isolated regions ice crystals are generated and grow large enough to begin to fall. As crystals collide, they aggregate into snowflakes which follow a trajectory determined by their fall speeds and the wind. Enter-ing lower elevations, they may fall into clouds of small subcooled droplets and continue growing by colliding with them. The clouds themselves would not be detected with most radar sets because the droplets are too small. Once the frozen particles fall through the $0°C$, they rapidly melt and accelerate. When they fall through low level clouds, they grow even larger by collision and coalescence with cloud droplets. If temperatures near the ground are below freezing, the precipitated particles remain in the form of snow.

Not all observed widespread cloud systems exhibit the well-defined upper-level streamers shown in Plate VII. In some systems there are pronounced bright bands with little evidence of anything above them.

This configuration probably occurs because the ice crystals in the clouds above the bright band are too small to give a detectable echo. When the crystals fall into the melting region, their reflectivities are increased by melting and possibly by rapid growth by coalescence.

Summary

Radar observations have led to a number of important findings. It has been clearly established that in many winter storms the rain reaching the ground has its origin at high altitudes in the form of ice crystals. On the other hand, the rainfall from convective clouds frequently is initiated in the absence of ice crystals.

When we have established which rain-producing process, the ice-crystal or coalescence process, is effective in particular types of clouds, we shall be in a better position to design successful cloud-seeding experiments. It is inevitable that sooner or later man will be able to modify clouds. Meteorologists all over the world are bending their efforts to find the answers as soon as possible. In this way they will make their contributions to helping to solve the world's water problems. Let us hope that when the time comes that more rain is produced, there will have been devised means to use it efficiently.

CHAPTER 7

THUNDERSTORMS, TORNADOES, AND HURRICANES*

Every year many people lose their lives, and millions of dollars' worth of property and crops are destroyed by the weather. Extended periods of too much or too little rain, blizzards and cold waves take part of the toll. But by far the most lethal and destructive storms are thunderstorms, tornadoes, and hurricanes. Thunderstorms may produce torrential rains and flash floods. They often are factories for hailstones which flatten crops. They act as giant generators which separate huge quantities of electric charge. When the voltage difference between the cloud and the ground becomes sufficiently great, the cloud discharges itself in a spasm of lightning. Finally, thunderstorms frequently cause gusty winds strong enough to produce great damage.

Tornadoes are almost always associated with thunderstorms but they occur much less frequently. When they do appear, they deal out death and destruction

* See *The Nature of Violent Storms* by Louis J. Battan, Science Study Series, S 19, for a more detailed discussion of thunderstorms, tornadoes, and hurricanes.

quickly and violently. They cause buildings to explode, and blow away even very heavy objects. A tornado is a narrow column of air whose velocity may exceed 300 mph. The whirling vortex may be less than 100 yards wide and last for only a few minutes. It is known that the pressure at the center of the whirl is quite low. In some cases it may be 10 per cent below the pressure outside the tornado funnel. When it suddenly passes over a building, the pressure outside drops quickly while the pressure inside changes slowly. This pressure difference leads to a strong force which may blow off the roof and blow out the walls just as if there were an explosion. The force can exceed 170 pounds per square foot of wall area. If this force is applied to a wall 8 feet high and 10 feet long, the total force is about 14,000 pounds, enough to push the wall violently outward. Once a building begins to collapse, the strong winds pick up the pieces and blow them through the air like shrapnel. Because of these violent effects tornadoes are the most feared of weather disturbances.

Hurricanes do tremendous damage year after year and sometimes lead to major losses of life. Unlike the tornado, which lasts only for a short period, the cyclones from the tropics last for days. The winds do not reach the terrifying magnitude of 300 mph, but they often do reach 100 and sometimes more than 150 mph. Also, these very strong winds may extend over a region of perhaps 50 miles across with winds exceeding 75 mph over a much larger area. Along coast lines approaching hurricanes generate monstrous waves which inundate low-lying terrain. Statistics show that the major loss of life in hurricanes occurs in drownings.

Meteorologists have been studying severe storms for many decades. One of the biggest stumbling blocks to better understanding and better predictions has been a lack of suitable observations, particularly in the case of tornadoes and hurricanes. In order to study these phenomena, it is necessary to be able to observe a large area at the same time. The tornado is small, but it lasts for a very short time, and it is impossible to predict exactly where one will form. Present procedures can forecast with fair accuracy that a tornado will form in an area perhaps 100 miles in diameter. If one wishes to study the tornado, it is necessary to be able to observe what is going on over the entire area.

Hurricanes are large and last for a long time. In order to obtain descriptions of the storm, one must be able to observe a large part of the storm quickly and in detail.

Instrumented airplanes capable of making many types of meteorological measurements are now being employed in research projects aimed at unraveling the mysteries of hurricanes, tornadoes, and thunderstorms. Ground-located and balloon-borne instruments also are in widespread use. And radar has been playing a prominent role.

Some important aspects of severe storms are the *location* and *intensity* of the rain showers as well as the *pattern* of the precipitation. Radar can supply this information better than can any other available instrument. In the past 15 years it has yielded new observations of great value.

Thunderstorms

In discussing convective rainfall in Chapter 6, we pointed out that thunderstorms frequently grow in stepwise fashion until they reach far into the atmosphere. Radar observations have shown that thunderstorms frequently reach altitudes of over 35,000 feet. Sometimes they go over 60,000 feet. It should be noted that the radar echoes represent the regions of large water or ice particles; the visual cloud usually extends several thousand feet higher than the echo top. The reason why the air inside the clouds ascends is that it is warmer and less dense than the air outside. As long as this condition prevails, upward acceleration continues. In general, once the cloud penetrates the base of the stratosphere, the cloud air rapidly becomes cooler and heavier than the outside air. This cooling leads to deceleration, and the cloud ceases to grow. Since the base of the stratosphere lies somewhere between 40,000 and 60,000 feet, this is the usual altitude range of the largest thunderstorms.

On some occasions the updraft speeds in thunderstorms are so high that even when the cloud air moves into the stratosphere and is subjected to a downward force, it continues moving upward for many thousands of feet. Some radar observations show thunderstorm tops extending as much as 16,000 feet (about 5 kilometers) into the stratosphere. For this to happen the updraft air must have extremely high momentum and this means high speeds. As a rule of thumb Bernard Vonnegut of A. D. Little, Inc., suggests that for each kilometer of penetration there must be a vertical velocity of about 10 meters per second. For stratosphere penetrations of 5 kilometers, the updraft speeds at the base of the stratosphere must be about 100 meters per second (about 220 mph). Such high vertical speeds greatly exceed the largest ones measured, but airplanes have made few cloud penetrations at altitudes where these high velocities might be expected. If the radar observations are correct, as they appear to be, airplanes flying at high altitudes should avoid thunderstorms. All airplanes except research airplanes do try to avoid them.

Since many installations such as airports are frequently under the threat of thunderstorms, it is important to be able to predict when one will move overhead. It is essential to be able to locate the storms and follow them as they grow, move, and dissipate. The fact that they grow and dissipate at the same time they move complicates the problem of predicting the future position of a storm.

A large white thundercloud is a vast region of minute water and ice particles which for the most part move with the wind. It has been found, however, that the cloud does not move exactly with the wind. In clouds with vertical motion some of the air actually blows around and "through" the cloud. On the upwind side, air enters the cloud, and on the downwind side, air leaves the cloud. The result is that the cloud moves at a slower speed than the wind.

Since thunderclouds are constantly changing in size, it sometimes appears as if their radar echoes are moving in a very erratic way. If the winds are light, the horizontal movements of the cloud and rain particles are small. If new thunderstorm clouds develop alongside the existing ones and merge with them, the center of the resulting echo can be displaced in almost any direction, depending on where the new clouds formed. Therefore, a knowledge of the upper-level wind direction on days when the winds are very light is of little help in forecasting whether or not a particular nearby thunderstorm is going to move over an airport. In such a situation it is necessary to keep the storm under constant radar surveillance and observe whether its boundaries are getting closer.

When the upper-level winds are strong, one can predict the movement of existing thunderstorms with satisfactory accuracy. It still is necessary to be alert to the development of new clouds which may make it appear as if the storm is moving faster or slower than the wind. Studies by a number of scientists have shown that the winds at an altitude of about 10,000 feet are well correlated with the movement of individual thunderstorm cells. This level is sometimes called the "steering level" because the winds at this level appear to steer the storms.

The isolated thunderstorm seen at a distance is often a beautiful sight with pure white flanks and a long tenuous anvil blowing off into a blue sky. On the other hand, the most dangerous thunderstorms are those that form in groups or lines. Sometimes the lines extend for hundreds of miles, and as they sweep

across the countryside, they lay down a curtain of
heavy rain, hail, and strong winds which may devas-
tate large regions in a matter of hours. Plate IX shows
a radar observation of a squall line with many thunderstorms. Lines such as these often can be followed
for hours, and their arrival can be predicted with fair
accuracy.

Lightning

The difference between a rainstorm and a thunderstorm, by definition, is that the latter produces thunder. If you hear thunder, you can be sure there has
been a lightning stroke. The lightning means, of
course, that the electric charges in the clouds have
built up to such great values that a large spark or arc
occurs. It is common to think of lightning as a gigan-
tic spark. We now know that lightning has many
characteristics of an electric arc; it is a fairly prolonged
surge of tremendous quantities of electric charge. The
quantity must be high enough to cause very high
temperatures and ionization of the air. We shall return to the ionization aspect of this problem in a later
section. First, let us consider some of the electrical
properties of a typical thunderstorm.

It has been found that, in general, a thundercloud
has a concentration of negative charge near the central portion of the cloud just above the freezing level.
The upper part of the cloud, on the other hand, is
predominantly positive. After the rain begins to fall,
a small positive charge center sometimes forms in the

bottom part of the cloud in the region of heavy rain. As the electric charge concentrated in these three regions continues to build up, the electric potential between them becomes larger and larger. When the potential reaches magnitudes of the order of 10,000 volts/cm, there is a sudden discharge through the air. It is said that at this point the voltage difference has reached the breakdown potential of air.

Since the centers of positive and negative charge may be separated by about two kilometers, one can easily calculate the voltage difference between the centers just before breakdown. It is given by the breakdown potential times the spacing of the centers, and therefore is about 2×10^9, or two billion, volts.

Once the breakdown begins it proceeds to completion in a few tenths of a second. In some respects this is a very short time, but when one considers the times commonly measured with modern electronic techniques, it is quite long. A great deal has been learned about lightning discharges through the use of electronic and photographic equipment. The cloud-to-ground stroke, in particular, has received concentrated attention in many parts of the world.

When the electric potential between cloud and ground reaches the breakdown potential, there is a sudden downward surge of electric charges. It proceeds about 150 feet at a velocity of about 31,000 miles/sec (5×10^7 meters/sec), or about one-sixth the speed of light. After this first downward step there is a pause of about 100 microseconds, and then a second surge occurs. In a series of steps the leading edge of the luminous region works its way toward the ground. This early part of the lightning stroke is called the *stepped leader*. It can be followed with special types of camera equipment and it has been found that it does not carry excessive quantities of charge. As a result it is not very bright.

When the stepped leader reaches within 50 to 100 feet of the ground, there is a sudden rush of a huge quantity of charge which appears to move up the leader stroke path. This is known as the *main stroke*. In less than 10 microseconds the electric current may reach a *peak value* of 200,000 amperes. The result is a brilliant flash of light which, in certain circumstances, can be seen more than 100 miles away. The main stroke proceeds upward at speeds of about 22,000 miles/sec (3.5×10^7 meters/sec).

In some cases there may be many main strokes which pass up the same lightning channel. Instead of the stepped leader which preceded the first main stroke, there are so-called *dart leaders* from the cloud to ground just before each main stroke. It has been found that a few exceptional lightning strokes have had more than thirty individual main strokes separated in time by a few hundredths of a second.

The human eye responds slowly to rapidly changing events. Hence, it is impossible to see the sequence of the stepped leader and main stroke, dart leader and main stroke, and so forth. When we see lightning, the flash of light is almost entirely a result of the main stroke or strokes. When one considers that the *average current* during each main stroke may be as high as 20,000 amperes, it becomes evident why lightning is so powerful and frightening. First there is the flash of light. The extreme currents heat up the air, cause expansion, and lead to pressure waves which propagate outward as sound waves. Since sound travels so much slower than light, the thunder will be heard after the lightning is seen. One may estimate the distance to a thunderstorm by counting the number of seconds which elapse between the sight of lightning and the sound of thunder and figuring the distance at one mile for each five seconds. For example, an elapsed time of fifteen seconds means the storm is about three miles away.

The damage done by lightning is largely a result of the heat it produces. Every year lightning-caused forest fires burn down thousands of acres of timberlands. Houses and barns are set afire. Sometimes trees and brick buildings are damaged because the sudden surge of heat causes the vaporization of water and a build-up of sufficient pressure to blow off the bark or blow out bricks.

An airliner flying through or near a thunderstorm may be struck by lightning. This has happened many times and is feared by most air travelers. Many years of research have resulted in protective measures which make metal airplanes virtually immune to serious damage by lightning. Basically the idea has been to make all outside surfaces good electrical conductors and to connect them electrically so that when lightning does strike, the charge remains on the skin. In the early days of aviation fires inside metal airplanes were sometimes started by high currents surging through the radio antennas. Proper connection of the antennas solved this problem. The use of wind shields which conduct electricity solved still another problem. When they were insulators, they were subject to shattering as arcs jumped across them. The damage done by lightning strokes to modern commercial and military aircraft usually amounts to a few little holes, perhaps ¼ inch in diameter, found in the wings or tail sections.

Probably the most dangerous aspect of lightning is the effect it has on the pilot's eyes. A sudden brilliant flash of light can cause temporary blinding. To overcome this difficulty it has long been a common practice to turn on the cockpit lights and to wear sunglasses; if there is a flash, the effects are minimized.

Until about 1950 it was not known whether radar could detect lightning strokes. At that time Myron G. H. Ligda at M.I.T. made some observations which proved conclusively that lightning did give an echo on a 10-cm radar set. His procedure was to point the radar beam at a thunderstorm and watch the echo on an A-scope. Before the lightning occurred, he received a normal echo from the precipitation particles. When the stroke passed through the radar beam, the radar echo rapidly increased in magnitude and then more slowly decreased. The lightning echo reached its maximum size in about one-half second and then decreased to zero in about one to five seconds. Other observers subsequently found average lightning echo durations of a few tenths of a second.

During the past ten years lightning has been detected on other types of radar sets. Most of the observations have been with wave lengths of 10, 23, or 50 cm. As a matter of fact, the number of lightning echoes observed has increased as longer wave equipment has been employed.

Why does radar detect a lightning stroke? Various possibilities have been suggested. The most widely accepted explanation is that the echo is a reflection of the incident radar waves by the free electrons in the lightning path. As noted earlier, the tremendous surge of current in the lightning channel causes an ionization of the gases in the channel. Large quantities of electrons are stripped off the gas atoms and molecules.

When a radio wave passes over the region of electrons, it causes them to oscillate with the same frequency as the radio waves. The oscillating electrons are similar in some respects to those which surge back and forth in a radar antenna and produce the radar waves in the first place. As a result, there is a re-radiation of radar energy back toward the radar.

Theoretical calculations can be made of the number of free electrons needed to produce the echoes. It is found that the longer the wave length the smaller the number of electrons. Ligda published a set of calculations which shows that for reflection of the incident energy, 10^{11} electrons per cubic centimeter are needed when a wave length of 3 cm is used. As one goes to wave lengths of 10, 23, and 50 cm, the critical number decreases to 10^{10}, 2×10^9, and 4×10^8 electrons per cubic centimeter respectively. The fact that fewer electrons are needed as one goes to longer wave lengths explains why lightning observations have become more numerous. In the late forties and early fifties 3-cm equipment was the most commonly used weather radar. In the last five years or so more observations have been taken at wave lengths greater than 20 cm.

Not only the magnitude of the radar echo from a lightning but its duration as well must be explained. David Atlas and F. J. Hewitt have studied this problem in some detail. They have explained signal strengths they measured in terms of free electrons, but their results do not agree. However, the differences can be resolved if their initial assumptions regarding the conditions in the lightning channel are made more alike.

The short duration of the lightning echo is to be expected in view of the fact that in the lightning channel there are large concentrations of free negative electrons and positive gas ions. In very short times the electrons and ions recombine to form neutral gas atoms and molecules of the type which existed before the lightning stroke. It can be shown that time periods of less than a second are long enough for sufficient recombinations to occur to cause the free electron concentration to fall so low that the echo disappears.

Atlas has obtained a number of radar observations such as the one shown in Plate X. It shows a lightning echo extending upward from the top of a thunderstorm. The lightning echo is prominent relative to the rest of the storm because of a photographic trick. It was first used by Ligda. First you take a negative that shows the observation of the precipitation and the lightning stroke. Then take a positive transparency of a radar observation a few seconds earlier that shows only the precipitation. The negative and the positive transparencies are superimposed on one another and a print is made. Since the precipitation echo appears on both films, light does not pass through the two transparencies very well and the echo becomes much weaker. On the other hand, the lightning stroke echo appears only on the negative and it prints as a white echo. This photographic technique is quite useful in emphasizing an image that appears and disappears rapidly and is partly merged with another image. Since lightning echoes last for less than a second, they would appear on only one scan of a radar set of the type whose scope picture is shown in Plate X, and they sometimes are hard to spot if one looks at only one picture at a time.

Ligda made a detailed examination of a large number of radar observations taken with 23-cm radar sets. He found that some lightning echoes extended for distances of well over fifty miles. This result was unexpected. Most meteorologists would not have guessed that a single stroke could be so extensive. However, the radar observations are conclusive.

Radar observations should be very helpful in developing a better understanding not only of the lightning discharge process, but also of the mechanism of electric charge separation.

Tornadoes

One reason why meteorologists are particularly interested in squall lines is that they sometimes spawn tornadoes. In some cases only a single funnel will be seen. More often, however, groups of them will be generated. The exact reasons why and how they develop are still matters of debate.

It has long been known that although most thunderstorms are not accompanied by tornadoes, tornadoes usually do not form unless there are thunderstorms. Until about fifteen years ago it was not even known where, relative to the thunderstorms, the funnel appeared. In 1953 scientists at the Illinois State Water Survey were fortunate to have their radar set in operation when a tornado passed within ten miles of their observatory. They succeeded in getting a series of photographs showing the formation of a peculiar echo which was definitely associated with the tornado. Some of their photographs are reproduced in Plate XI. The illustrations show a large thunderstorm echo which moved toward the east-northeast at a range of ten to twenty miles from the radar set. On the rear right side of the echo a narrow finger protruded southward and the end rotated counterclockwise to form an echo resembling the numeral 6. A detailed analysis by Tetsuya Fujita of the University of Chicago revealed that several tornado funnels were generated on the southernmost edge of the hook-shape echo.

After the publication of these photographs other investigators uncovered more examples of similar echoes accompanied by tornadoes. In general, the hooks were located on the rear-right flanks of thunderstorm echoes. Unfortunately, it was found also that most thunderstorm echoes that accompanied tornadoes did not have the distinctive hook. The analyses led to the conclusion that when the hook was present, one could conclude that a tornado was present but that the absence of the hook did not mean that there was no tornado. Other echo characteristics were found to be associated with tornado-bearing thunderstorms, but none was found sufficiently reliable to be adopted as a positive means of tornado detection. These results have been discouraging, but the search for positive means for tornado identification is continuing.

During the last few years studies have been made of a radar technique new in meteorology—Doppler radar. While the conventional radar set measures the location and size of a target, a Doppler radar measures the speed at which a target moves toward or away from the radar set. The Doppler system measures the change of the frequency of the radar waves resulting from the movement of the target. In elementary physics the Doppler effect is usually explained in terms of sound waves. The sound of a train whistle changes as the train approaches and leaves a station because the movement of the train leads to an apparent change of the frequency of the sound waves reaching the ears of the observer. By measuring the changes in frequency of the radar waves one can calculate the speed of the radar target.

There was speculation that a Doppler radar would be able to locate tornadoes because they would cause water drops to move at high speeds. The U. S. Weather Bureau has been employing 3-cm continuous-wave Doppler radar for testing this idea. This type of radar set is one which transmits a continuous stream of radar waves rather than short pulses. A target would reflect a continuous stream of radio waves. Since it is impossible to measure the time elapsed between transmission and reception of the radar energy, it is not possible to measure the range to the targets, but this radar can measure the speed of the targets which, in this case, are the back-scattering particles associated with a tornado. The Weather Bureau found that in one tornado the Doppler frequency shift corresponded to a wind speed of 205 mph. One observation can hardly be considered conclusive, but this technique certainly offers some hope.

Hurricanes

Hurricanes occur over tropical oceans in many regions of the world. They are called by various names in different parts of the world (for example, "typhoons" and "willy-willys"), but they all form in more or less the same way and have similar properties. In hurricanes of the northern hemisphere the winds blow counterclockwise; the reverse is true in the southern hemisphere. As one proceeds toward the center of a hurricane, the winds increase until one reaches a point perhaps 20 to 40 miles from the center. At smaller distances from the center, the winds become lighter and lighter.

A very distinctive feature of a hurricane is the "eye." This is a central region where the winds are not strong and there are few clouds. When a storm moves overhead, the eye becomes strikingly evident as heavy rains and strong winds are replaced by good weather. However, the calm lasts only for a short time, perhaps an hour or two, before the rear part of the storm strikes.

Radar observations have taught us a number of things about hurricanes. They have shown that in many of these tropical storms the rain showers are well organized. The most frequent pattern consists of series of spiral bands (Plate XII). Henry V. Senn and Homer W. Hiser at the University of Miami found that the bands of precipitation echoes closely follow the curve represented mathematically by the so-called logarithmic spiral. From a comparison of the actual spiral with the precise mathematical spiral, one can obtain the center of the hurricane. This technique for locating and tracking the center of hurricanes has been found quite useful.

Not all hurricanes exhibit well-defined spirals. As shown by Charles L. Jordan at Florida State University, in some storms there is a ring of echo around the center of the storm. In one hurricane the echo was found to extend nearly vertically to about 60,000 feet.

As pointed out earlier, the individual thunderstorm echoes tend to follow the winds at the 10,000-foot level, particularly when the winds are strong. Thus, if one tracks the movement of echoes, one can obtain information about the winds in hurricanes. Senn and Hiser have done this tracking and have succeeded in plotting profiles of wind velocity around a number of storms. When information of this type is combined with other observations obtained by aircraft and more conventional equipment, it will become possible to describe accurately the properties of hurricanes and to develop more complete theories of their behavior.

The problem of predicting the future movement and development of a hurricane is a complicated one. Meteorological measurements over a large part of the northern hemisphere must be used if a forecast is to be made for a period of as long as two days in advance. A hurricane can be considered a swirling vortex in a large sea of air whose motion in one place is affected by motions in other parts of the atmosphere. As the forecast period becomes shorter, a smaller region must be considered. However, for all forecasts it is essential that the present and immediately past positions be known. With a network of radar sets this information can be obtained quickly and accurately once the hurricane moves within the range of the radar sets. In order to protect the southern and eastern parts of the United States from a surprise attack, radar stations have been installed along the Gulf and Atlantic coasts. The likelihood of a hurricane's approaching undetected is small indeed.

and more... that region R will become possible to describe accurately the properties of but difficult... and to develop more complete theories of their behavior.

The problem of predicting the future movement and development of a hurricane is a difficult one. Radar... measurements over a large part of the northern hemisphere... if a forecast is to be made for a period of as little as two days in advance. A hurricane can be considered a swirling vortex of air whose motion in one place is affected by the motion in other parts of the atmosphere. As the forecast period becomes shorter, a smaller region must be considered. However, for all forecasts it is essential that the present and immediately past positions be known within a network of radar sites. This information can be obtained quickly and accurately once the hurricane moves within the range of the radar sets. In order to protect the southern and eastern parts of the United States from a hurricane attack, radar stations have been seen installed along the Gulf and Atlantic coasts. The likelihood of a hurricane approaching undetected is small indeed.

CHAPTER 8

RADAR AIDS THE PILOT

The instrument panel of a modern airliner is an array, rank on rank, of dials and indicators which all play an important part in the operation and navigation of the airplane. Before adding another instrument, it is necessary to show that it will serve an important function. When radarscopes were first brought into cockpits, some pilots were skeptical, but just a little experience proved that radar was useful indeed. For the first time it became possible to "see" through clouds and locate areas with severe weather.

Some meteorologists proposed late in the forties that airborne radar would be a valuable instrument for commercial airliners because of its weather-observing abilities. However, the airline industry did not move recklessly. Existing airborne radar sets had some problems. The available sets were not suitable for airline use. For the most part they had been designed for military purposes, such as bombing or directing gunfire. In general, the sets were quite heavy because they had fairly complicated functions to perform. Some weighed 400 pounds or more. Further-

more, they were very costly to buy and to maintain.
There were other more fundamental problems. There
was no commercial aircraft experience to demonstrate that radar would do what had been claimed.
Also, there was the question of the proper specifications of a radar designed specifically for the airlines.

During the period 1947 to 1949 research on the
value of radar observations by the National Advisory
Committee on Aeronautics, which is now part of the
National Aviation and Space Agency, was begun.
The scientists of this group compared observations
of thunderstorm turbulence measured with airplanes
and thunderstorm echoes seen on ground radar sets.
The measurements had been obtained by a research
group called the Thunderstorm Project, which was
directed by Horace R. Byers of the University of Chicago. Both groups, N.A.C.A. and the Thunderstorm
Project, reached the conclusion that radar could lead
to a marked reduction in the turbulence to which
planes were subjected. Radar could supply accurate
location of thunderstorms and other regions of bad
weather.

In 1949 American Airlines carried out a series of
flight tests with a military 3-cm radar set with the aim
of testing its value for various purposes. The specific
questions they hoped to answer were the following:
Could radar help the pilot avoid regions of severe turbulence and hail? Could radar help to reduce the
hazards of collisions with mountains or other terres-
trial flight obstructions?

The radar set employed by American Airlines had

a new electronic circuit invented by a young scientist, David Atlas, who was working with the Air Force. He had predicted, in 1947, that the most severe turbulence in a thunderstorm would occur in regions where there was a large difference of echo intensity over a small distance. In more technical terms, this means that large gradients of echo intensity were associated with turbulence. Atlas devised a system for displaying on a single PPI enough information to permit direct indication of the echo gradient.

When you look at an echo on a PPI, the outer edge of the echo represents the minimum power which the radar can detect. If the returned signal had been less than this amount, no echo would have appeared on the scope. If the amount of power had been greater, the echo would have been brighter than appears on the actual picture. The amount of power giving an echo that can just barely be seen is called the *threshold of detection*. The line represented by the threshold is called an *isoecho contour*, because it is a line along which the echo power has the same value. If a radar set is properly calibrated, one can adjust the threshold to any particular level.

Every radar set has a so-called *gain control*. It is equivalent to a volume control on a radio. By turning it up one increases the amplification of the received signals. As a result, the sounds from a radio become louder, and in some cases some weak stations will become audible for the first time. The radar gain control can do the same thing with radar signals.

If the gain control on a radar is turned down, only

the stronger signals will give an echo. If, in the case of the echo shown in Fig. 15, the gain were reduced to such a value that the threshold corresponded to the power represented by the line numbered 2, the PPI would show an echo much smaller than the original one. If one could present thresholds 1 and 2 simultaneously, the region of maximum echo gradient could be seen immediately. In our example, it is found on the right-hand edge of the echo in the region where the threshold lines are closest. This is the region where the most turbulence would be found.

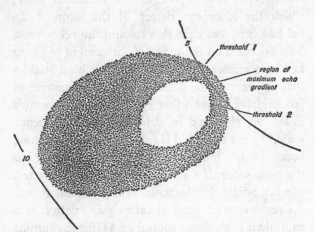

FIG. 15. *Sketch of echo as it would appear on the PPI of a radar set having isoecho contour mapping. See the text for a discussion of this illustration.*

Isoecho Contour Mapping

Atlas derived a system for simultaneously presenting two levels of equal echo intensity. The scheme is called *isoecho contour mapping*. In principle, two circuits are used to detect two threshold values. Both would normally put out signals positive in sign. If they were added together and then channeled to a PPI, the usual type of echo would be displayed. Around the edges it would be faint, and it would be increasingly bright as the point of maximum rainfall was reached somewhere in the inner region of the echo.

In contour mapping, the output signal for the circuit adjusted to represent only the strong signal is first *inverted in sign*. Then it is added to the output of the circuit with the lower threshold. In regions where the negative signals from one circuit are added to the positive signals from the other, there is a cancellation of the two signals. This cancellation occurs in the region bounded by the isoecho contour representing the heavier rain. The final result is an echo with a "hole" on the inside. The outer edge of the echo corresponds to threshold 1 and the edge of the hole corresponds to threshold 2.

Plate XIII shows two radar photographs taken with an airborne radar set. The one on the left shows the normal type of echo appearance. The photograph on the right was taken a short time later and shows the effects of the isoecho contour circuitry. The dark areas within the echoes 10 miles to the northwest and 17 miles to the northeast show regions of heavy rain and strong gradients of echo intensity. These echoes would be expected to contain more severe turbulence than the echoes to the southwest. In addition, it can be concluded that the turbulence in the echo 10 miles to the northwest would be worst in the south and west parts because the gradients of echo intensity are greatest there.

The work by American Airlines led to the conclusion that an airborne radar with contour mapping could help a pilot avoid severe turbulence. They were not able to demonstrate that radar could be used successfully to avoid hail or ground collision.

In the early fifties United Air Lines installed a 5.5-cm radar set built by Radio Corporation of America in one of their airplanes and set out on an extensive series of test flights. The photographs in Plate XIII were taken with the United radar set. The specifications for the radar were formulated by the airline on the basis of recommendations made by a panel of airline and radar experts. The radar set was the first airborne radar specifically designed for mapping weather. Henry T. Harrison, who directed the research, and his associates conclusively demonstrated that radar could do what was claimed. It could help the pilot to locate and avoid regions of severe turbulence. By flying around them, the pilot also could avoid damaging hail. (See Chapter 4.) United Air Lines led the way in equipping its airplanes with radar. Other airlines quickly followed the lead. A recent ruling by the Federal Aviation Agency stated that by

1961 all commercial airplanes above a certain size must be equipped with airborne radar.

It was pointed out earlier that radar equipment existing in the late forties was not satisfactory for airline use. This problem has been solved to a very large extent. First of all, the operation of the radar systems was simplified so that they could be easily operated and maintained. To this end the capabilities of the radar set were limited to those functions considered essential. Consequently, the weight of the radar system was reduced. The total weight of the radar sets now in use is about 150 pounds.

One question which still has not been resolved is: What is the optimum wave length? Some airlines use 3-cm equipment because it can detect storms at great distances and can produce a narrower beam width than longer wave length equipment. Other airlines employ 5.5-cm equipment. Although the maximum detection range is smaller and the beam width is larger than with 3-cm sets, the longer waves suffer less attenuation by heavy rain. As a result, they can see through longer distances of heavy rain. It is worth noting that virtually all airline radar antennas are located in the nose of the airplane. As a result, the size of the antenna (about 2 to 3 ft in diameter) is limited by the fact that the configuration of the nose must be rounded and properly shaped. A molded dome called a radome houses the antenna. It is made of a material through which the radar waves can pass freely without absorption. Since this section is usually not painted a distinctive color, it is sometimes not easy to tell whether or not the nose section contains a radar antenna. However, many airlines are still rightly proud of these radar sets and have prominently labeled the airplanes "radar equipped."

Some New Developments

The airborne radar sets currently used by commercial airplanes have antennas which scan around a vertical axis. Thus they give the conventional type of PPI information. It has been proposed by the author that they be modified so that vertical scanning be possible when the pilot wants information in the vertical plane ahead of the aircraft. Information obtained from this type of operation can be quite valuable in certain situations.

Let us say, for example, that an airliner is flying toward a line of thunderstorms some thirty or forty miles ahead. If the antenna were switched from horizontal scanning to vertical scanning, the scope would automatically present a picture of height versus range. The altitude of the thunderstorm echoes could be read directly off the scope. (See Plate XIV.) One can obtain information about the tops of thunderstorms with the conventional scanning, but it is time-consuming. As pointed out in Chapter 7, the vertical extent of a thunderstorm is a measure of its severity.

If one were to use vertical scanning with a radar set having contour mapping, he could quickly obtain both the maximum heights and an estimate of maximum echo intensity. This information would make it possible to draw conclusions about the likelihood of hail, and possibly, of tornadoes.

Vertically scanning radar also would make it an easy matter to locate the bright band when one is present. Its existence would indicate that serious aircraft icing was not likely. Icing is the accumulation of ice on airplane parts caused when waterdrops at subfreezing temperatures strike the airplane and freeze. Aircraft icing seldom represents a hazard to modern airliners, but occasionally it does cause some problems. When there is a pronounced bright band, the region above the freezing level is mostly filled with snow and ice crystals. When the precipitation is in this form, icing is usually not serious.

Another thing that a vertically scanning radar can do is to give a profile of the topography of the ground in the vertical plane through which the antenna is scanning. In the past there have been disastrous accidents in which airplanes have flown into the mountains. In some cases the accidents might have occurred even if the pilots knew the location of the mountain. The airplane may have been out of control. However, in others the mountains were hidden from view in clouds or fog and were not known to be present. A technique for observing the terrain as an airplane makes an approach into a cloud-hidden airfield would reduce the possibilities of running into high ground, particularly in regions where the navigational and radar landing aids are not well developed.

The idea of employing vertically scanning airborne radar in commercial airplanes is still fairly new and untested, but, because of its advantages, it should be investigated in detail before too many years have passed.

CHAPTER 9

RADAR SEES THE EARTH
AND ANGELS

When some of the outgoing radar energy strikes the
earth, part of it is reflected back and one sees echoes
of the ground. This result is reasonable and easy to
understand. On the other hand, radarscopes sometimes show echoes from regions in the sky which are
absolutely clear. In the early days of radar these
echoes were given such interesting names as "ghost
echoes," "phantom echoes," and "angel echoes." The
last one has caught on, and it is common to hear
echoes which cannot be easily explained called angels. We now have some good ideas about the source
of these mysterious echoes. Let us first examine the
ground echoes and come back to the angels.

Echoes from the Ground

Almost all PPI pictures from ground-based radar
sets show some echoes from the ground at very short
ranges. They are often called "ground clutter" because they almost never serve a useful purpose. In-

stead, they clutter the picture and make it difficult to clearly identify targets, such as airplanes, which move close to the radar set.

The reason why ground clutter is common is that only small quantities of power are needed to return a detectable signal from good reflecting or scattering surfaces located at very short ranges. Small amounts of power are radiated over a wide angle even with radar antennas producing narrow beams. When we say that a radar set has a beam width of 2 degrees, we do not mean that all the power is concentrated within the 2 degrees around the axis. In fact, with a typical radar antenna, about 80 per cent of the total outgoing power is contained within the beam. The remaining 20 per cent is transmitted at various angles away from the beam axis. When one considers the large range of angles over which the 20 per cent is distributed, it becomes clear that the concentration of power per unit area is low indeed. As a result, few echoes are received, except as reflections from the main beam, when target ranges greater than perhaps ten to fifteen miles are involved. This explains why only nearby ground areas normally appear as ground echoes.

On some occasions the ground clutter extends out from its normal location to very large ranges. In some extreme cases ground targets 400 to 500 miles away have been observed. This seems strange. It would have been reasonable to assume that a narrow beam of electromagnetic waves radiated horizontally would propagate almost horizontally along a straight line (sometimes called the "line of sight"). As a matter of fact, radio waves in the atmosphere almost never travel along a straight line. In a free space they would do so, but the atmosphere certainly is not free space. The variations of pressure, temperature, and humidity are important factors in causing the radar beams to be "bent."

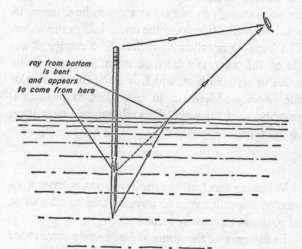

ray from bottom is bent and appears to come from here

FIG. 16. *The ray of light from the bottom of the pencil changes direction as it emerges from the water. As a result, the pencil looks shorter than it actually is. The bending of the light ray occurs because the refractive index of the air is less than that of water.*

The bending of light rays is easily demonstrated. Take a pencil and dip part of it in water. (See Fig. 16.) When you look down at the stick from the side, it will appear shorter than it actually is. This happens because the light rays being reflected from the pencil

are deflected at the surface of the water. The change
of direction of a light beam can be explained by con-
sidering light as a wave whose velocity is changed as
the wave passes from one medium to another. When
a light wave passes from water to air, for example,
the velocity of light increases. The amount of the increase is enough to cause the wave to be directed in
a different direction from the one it had in the water.
The bending is called *refraction*. The change of angle of the wave is related to a quantity called the
index of refraction, n, which is equal to the ratio of
the velocity of light, *c,* in free space to the actual
velocity, *v,* of the wave. This relation can be written
in the form

$$n = \frac{c}{v} \qquad (4)$$

When an electromagnetic wave passes from a region of one value of *n* to a region of a smaller value
of *n,* the wave velocity increases.

In the case of the atmosphere the refractive index
normally decreases slowly with altitude. A radar wave
directed upward at an angle of 45 degrees, for example, would gradually increase in speed as it went to
higher elevations. At the same time it would be bent
downward. Again, it should be noted that the change
of speed is very small, and the wave can never reach
the speed of light in free space.

The refractive index of air can be calculated from
an equation involving pressure, temperature, and humidity. Since all three factors vary, the refractive index varies. A typical value near the ground is about
1.0003 and the rate at which it decreases with height

in an average atmosphere is about 4×10^{-8} per meter of altitude. It can be shown that in such an atmosphere a radar beam transmitted horizontally would be bent downward and follow a circle whose radius is about 1.3 times the radius of the earth. As shown in Fig. 16a, an outgoing horizontally transmit-

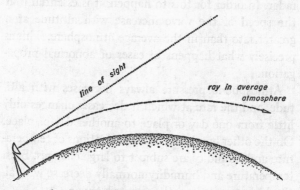

FIG. 16a. *In an average atmosphere the refractive index as far as radar waves are concerned decreases with height. As a result the radar rays are bent downward as shown. On the other hand, light rays travel along a straight line.*

ted beam would gradually move farther and farther away from the surface of the earth, and the distance away would not increase as fast as it would if the ray followed a straight line.

How does it happen, then, that on some occasions ground targets are seen at ranges of many hundreds of miles?

The situation we have been discussing refers to average or so-called normal conditions in the atmosphere. Sometimes the variations with altitude of temperature and humidity are not normal. It is in such instances that one obtains abnormal propagation.

Fig. 16a shows the radar beam normally bent downward by a small amount. If the bending could be increased enough, the beam could be made to strike the surface of the earth at some distance from the radar. In order for this to happen, it is essential that the speed of the wave increase with altitude at a greater rate than in the average atmosphere. This is precisely what happens in cases of abnormal propagation.

Atmospheric pressure always decreases with altitude, and the rate at which it decreases changes only little from one day or place to another day or place. On the other hand, the vertical variations of temperature and humidity are subject to large changes. Both temperature and humidity normally decrease with altitude, but sometimes the reverse is true.

An examination of the equation for the refractive index shows that it decreases most rapidly with height when temperature increases with altitude while the humidity decreases rapidly with altitude. Various meteorological processes can lead to these conditions. The most striking effects occur when warm, dry air moves over a body of cooler water. The water reduces the air temperature close to the surface and produces a so-called *temperature inversion*—that is, a condition where the temperature increases with height. Evaporation from the water surface adds humidity to the lowest layers of the air. In this circumstance one can expect abnormal propagation; the radar waves can follow a path such as shown in Fig. 17. The wave may become trapped in a narrow layer close to the earth and can be "reflected" successively from the upper part of the layer and the earth's surface. The layer is sometimes called a *duct* because the energy is trapped inside.

Conditions of the type just described are sometimes encountered in the Mediterranean region when warm, dry air from Africa moves over the sea. In

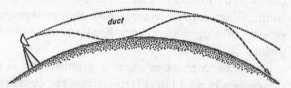

FIG. 17. *When the temperature increases and humidity decreases rapidly near the earth's surface, a so-called "duct" is formed. The duct traps the radar waves and causes them to follow a path such as the one shown. As a result ground echoes may be seen at great ranges.*

World War II some of the most pronounced cases of abnormal propagation occurred in this area. Ground targets many hundreds of miles away produced strong echoes.

When the night sky is clear and the ground moist, radiation from the earth's surface can lead to low-level temperature inversions and the proper humidity distribution to produce ducts and abnormal propagation. Occasionally these ducts also affect television transmissions. Chicago viewers may pick up Milwaukee stations, for example. Of course, the radio waves used in television are much longer than those used in conventional radar sets, but they follow the same laws of refraction.

Various other types of meteorological conditions can also lead to the temperature and humidity distributions which will produce peculiar ground clutter patterns. Radar operators must be aware of all the possibilities in order to interpret accurately the echo patterns on the scope. Often the appearance of a ground echo will be very similar to that from a rainstorm. When conditions are ripe for abnormal propagation, all suspicious echoes need special investigation.

One way to check whether a distant echo is a shower or a ground target is to increase the elevation angle at which the antenna is scanning. It can be shown that if the antenna beam is pointing at an angle more than about 2 degrees above the horizon, the downward bending will not be sufficient to cause the outgoing beam to strike the ground. This is true even where the refractive index decreases with height with abnormal rapidity.

It might be asked, if this is true, Why not keep the antenna elevation angle at 2 degrees or greater at all times? This can certainly be done in some cases, but if one wishes to see rain showers at long distances it is necessary to point the antenna at the lowest possible angle, preferably horizontal. Otherwise the radar beam will pass over the tops of many showers and thunderstorms which would be detected at a lower elevation angle.

In summary, it can be stated that the surface of the earth is a good back-scatterer of radar energy.

Normally, atmospheric conditions are such that the pattern of ground clutter is restricted to short ranges. On the other hand, when temperature increases rapidly with height and humidity decreases rapidly with height, ducts can be formed which trap the radar energy near the earth's surface and lead to ground echoes at long ranges.

Angels

In 1940 Albert W. Friend reported the first detection of angel echoes. He pointed a radar set vertically and detected echoes that could not be associated with any visible objects. The sky was clear; he could not attribute the echo to cloud or raindrops. Friend suggested that the radar energy was being reflected from a layer of air through which the temperature or humidity or both were changing rapidly with height. Since those first observations about twenty years ago, there have been many observations of angel echoes. A common type is illustrated in Plate XVI. Sometimes one finds a layer of moderately spaced dots. In other cases there are several layers. On some occasions the dots are widely separated.

Before looking at other types of angel echoes, let us briefly examine the suggested explanations for echoes from a clear sky.

It has been proposed that angel echoes could be produced by swarms of insects or birds too far away to be seen but large enough to give an echo. Vernon G. Plank of the Air Force Cambridge Research

Center made a detailed study of a large group of angel echoes observed in the Boston area with a 1.25-cm radar set. He investigated the habits of the insects and birds likely to be found around Boston. His conclusion was that on some of the days on which angels were observed, it would have been impossible for sufficient numbers of insects or birds to be present to account for the echoes. On the other hand, conditions on all the days were favorable for the production of large gradients of refractive index of the air. As already noted, refractive index of the air depends mostly on temperature and humidity. The index decreases as temperature increases and humidity decreases. As a result, if there were a region of rising humid air surrounded by dry air, there would be a large gradient of refractive index at the boundary of the rising air.

Plank's work failed to convince some scientists that the bird explanation did not account for some of the angel echoes. For example, Robert E. Richardson of M.I.T. has presented evidence that a single sea gull could give a radar echo. He has pointed out that a sea gull could be considered to have a radar cross-sectional area equal to about 100 cm^2. Such a target area could lead to a strong echo on a radar set at ranges greater than twenty miles. It was further noted that a single bird within a beam volume which might be a mile wide could easily escape the notice of an observer. On the basis of this work and other observations to be discussed later, it must be concluded that some angel echoes are caused by birds. It also appears that some angels could not reasonably be explained this way.

There is no doubt that if the refractive index changes by a large amount over a short distance, there can be a reflection back to the radar of sufficient power to give a detectable echo. According to various theories which have been developed, very large gradients of refractive index are needed. Unfortunately, the instruments available for directly measuring refractive index do not respond fast enough. The best instrument for this purpose is called the *microwave refractometer*, developed at the University of Texas. This device has been mounted on airplanes and many observations have been made. It has been found, for example, that large gradients of refractive index occur across the boundaries of convective clouds which are growing in a dry atmosphere. These large changes can be ascribed in good part to large differences in the humidity. The airborne refractometer could not measure changes of refractive index over distances smaller than about 90 cm. According to the present theories on the subject, a 3-cm radar set should not detect angel echoes unless there are large changes of refractive index over a distance of the order of 5 cm. Perhaps, with the more rapidly responding instruments now under development, sufficiently large gradients will be found.

Although there is little theoretical support, the observational evidence to be presented in the following sections suggests that in some cases angel echoes probably are caused by high gradients of refractive index.

Let us consider various types of angel echoes.

On days when convective clouds are present, various types of angels are sometimes seen. Under the clouds, in the rising clear air, small "point" or "column" echoes occur briefly. They are similar to the individual echoes in Plate XVI. Some scientists have suggested that they are caused by refractive index changes across the boundaries of the thermals feeding air into the cloud base. An alternative explanation is that the echoes are caused by birds flying in the thermals and feeding on insects and other types of food lifted in the rising air.

A type of angel echo of large extent and long duration has been found ahead of squall lines. Plate XV shows an example of a long thin echo in front of a group of large thunderstorms. From many observations it has been established that these lines of angel echoes occur in regions where there are few clouds or none. They are associated with the leading edge of a mass of cool air blowing out from the thunderstorms. As the edge of the cool air passes overhead, the temperature drops rapidly and the relative humidity rises. Some scientists have ascribed the echoes to refractive index changes. On the other hand, W. G. Harper at Imperial College in London favors the idea that the line of echoes are caused by the reflection of radar waves by birds. In at least one well-documented case he used a telescope to watch the region of the atmosphere from which angel echoes were being received. He saw many swifts darting in and out of the field of view of the telescope. He concluded that they were feeding on insects carried upward by rising air. It has long been known that as the cool air under a thunderstorm spreads out, it forces air up its leading edge. Once the air begins to rise, thermals may be produced. Harper's explanation is reasonable but it still is not certain that it explains all lines of angel echoes.

A most interesting echo is called the "ring angel." It was first observed by Floyd C. Elder, at the University of Michigan; he was using a 23-cm radar set. Elder has a long series of photographs taken at intervals of about ten seconds. When they are run as a movie, it is seen that the rings develop as small circles and expand at speeds of about 50 mph. In some cases as many as four rings formed at the same place and spread out at intervals of about 4 minutes. In a motion picture the sequence resembled the pattern one sees on a calm lake when he throws in a stone. Elder expressed the tentative opinion that the explanation for these echoes was linked to refractive index gradients. However, a number of scientists have proposed the bird theory again. They have suggested that birds sometimes roost in great numbers and that when disturbed they may take off and fly outward in all directions. In a few cases there have been observations of ring angels and simultaneous observations of birds in the proper places at the appropriate times. If all the ring angels, particularly those of Elder, were caused by birds, one would have to conclude that the flying habits of birds are more organized and carefully navigated than one would have expected.

Another type of angel echo which has received considerable study, especially by David Atlas, is one produced by the sea breeze. Along the coasts of fairly large bodies of water it is common, in the summer, for the wind to blow toward the water during the night but toward the coast during the afternoon. This type of circulation is brought about because the sun's rays heat the land more than the sea. When the land air becomes sufficiently warm, it begins to rise and is replaced by a breeze from over the water. In some regions of the world the shift occurs regularly and is welcomed with pleasure because of its cooling effects.

It has been found that the cool air is perhaps 2000 to 3000 ft deep and that it advances over the land as a large body. Atlas and his co-workers used a 1.25-cm radar to observe the advance of the sea breeze moving over the Massachusetts shore line. They observed very distinct echoes from a cloudless region which could be associated with the leading edge of the sea breeze. It approached at about 9 mph, and when it moved overhead, the temperature suddenly dropped and the humidity rose. They concluded, after an extensive analysis, that the sea breeze angels were caused by refractive index gradients.

In summary, it should be remembered that many times radar sets at all wave lengths pick up echoes coming from regions clear of clouds and other visible objects. However, the fact that a single large bird like a sea gull can give an echo when it is located more than 20 miles away means that birds may be causing the echoes even though they cannot be seen. If one had a line of birds spaced at intervals of one-half to a mile apart, it would be possible to obtain a line of echoes. As long as one bird was in the radar beam, there would be an echo.

On some occasions, the configuration of the angel echoes, their duration, pattern and speed of movement make it unlikely that the echoes could have been caused by birds. In these cases it is probable that the echoes were caused by reflections of radar energy by regions of the atmosphere where the refractive index changed by a large amount over a small distance.

and echoes along to see him, and in the radar band,
there would be an echo.

On some occasions, the reputation of the angel
echoes flew. Birds are patient and speed of movement and air turbulence, and the ... there could have
been caused by birds. In these cases it is probable
that the echoes were caused by reflections of radar
energy by regions of the atmosphere where the refractive index changed by a large amount over a small
distance.

CHAPTER 10

SOME SPECIAL RADAR
PROCEDURES AND APPLICATIONS

Since radar entered the domain of weather observing
and forecasting, scientists concerned with meteorological problems have directed their attention to the
development of special techniques for solving specific
important problems.

An excellent example of a new electronic development for dealing with a meteorological problem is
found in a radarscope presentation called Constant
Altitude Plan Position Indicator or CAPPI for short.
When studying large storm systems such as extensive
squall lines, hurricanes, or winter cyclones, it is desirable to be able to observe the pattern of precipitation at a particular altitude. It is not possible with a
conventional radar. Even if the radar antenna is
pointed horizontally as it scans in a circle, the fact
that the earth curves means that as the range increases the radar detects echoes at high elevations.

Scientists at McGill University, under the direction
of J. Stewart Marshall, have solved this dilemma.
They have developed a system in which the antenna
elevation angle increases in steps while a "ring" of

echo information is extracted at a range which decreases with each step. By properly selecting the interval at which the elevation angle is stepped upward, and the interval at which the range is stepped to lower values, one obtains a series of rings at about the same altitude. (See Fig. 18.) The rings are com-

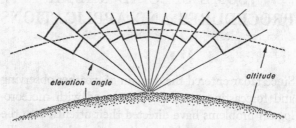

FIG. 18. *Consider a radar set with the antenna rotating around a vertical axis. By varying the elevation angle of the antenna in steps and properly selecting a range interval at each step, one obtains a series of rings which, in cross section, look like those shown here. Combining the information of all the rings gives a PPI picture at a fixed altitude above the ground.*

bined electronically to produce a PPI picture representing echoes at a particular altitude. One may select any altitude up to 50,000 feet. A more representative one is 10,000 feet because most precipitating clouds pass through this altitude.

If one had a network of radar sets spaced perhaps 100 to 200 miles apart, it would be possible with the CAPPI system to obtain a complete picture of large storms. If one did not have the new system, it would be difficult to tell if observed changes of echo size and intensity were caused by differences in range or differences in altitude. At McGill University CAPPI observations have been used to make important studies of the patterns of rain and snow showers. However, this scheme, which was proposed only a few years ago, has just begun to be used. It offers tremendous possibilities for investigating a large group of problems which could not have been tackled earlier.

Another idea proposed by the McGill group (in 1958) also has great merit. In an earlier chapter we discussed the importance of measuring the intensity of the echo. In Chapter 8 the isoecho contour mapping was cited as a widely used technique for obtaining two thresholds of echo intensity on the same PPI. A new type of echo presentation called "stepped-gray scale" of echo intensity has been developed which makes it possible to identify up to five or more levels of echo intensity.

As we know, a normal PPI echo of a rainstorm appears as an image varying in brightness from near black to near white. The variation in brightness is fairly smooth. The echo that can just barely be detected corresponds to the minimum detectable signal. The brightest part of the echo corresponds often to the maximum signal level the radar can measure—namely, the echo that saturates the radar receiver. In order to find out intermediate levels of echo intensity one could use a photo densitometer to measure the brightness of the echo. But before this information could be interpreted in terms of the power backscattered from the rain, it would be necessary to know the response of the film to the light from the scope and to use careful developing procedures. These difficulties make this procedure impractical.

The stepped-gray scale idea overcomes these difficulties. Instead of presenting a continuous range of

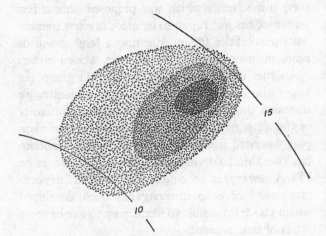

FIG. 19. *Sketch of the appearance of an echo on the scope of a radar set which employs stepped-gray scale echo presentation. Instead of having the echo brightness change gradually from near-black to near-white, the echo brightness jumps in steps. Each of the steps corresponds to a known threshold of echo intensity. As a result one could draw lines of equal echo intensity.*

brightness, a number of discrete shades of gray are employed. To accomplish this feat a special amplifier circuit must be used in the radar receiver. An echo might appear as shown in Fig. 19. Each shade of gray corresponds to a known average power level. With this scheme it is possible to draw isoecho contours, and one can note regions of large echo gradients easily and quickly.

Still another new technique of obtaining information about the echo intensity distribution makes use of a scope giving the "profile of average reflectivity" along a horizontal or vertical line. Edwin Kessler III of the Air Force Cambridge Research Center, who devised this technique, calls the presentation a PAR-scope. It can be used to obtain the vertical profile of average echo intensity through a thunderstorm, for example. It permits a direct observation of the altitudes at which maximum echo intensity occurs as well as the magnitude of the signal. As pointed out in Chapter 4, a knowledge of the vertical extent of a thunderstorm and the maximum echo intensity allows one to draw conclusions about the likelihood of hail. The PAR-scope gives this information directly. It also permits you to study the growth and spread of all types of precipitation particles and therefore is of value in studying cloud and rainfall processes.

Shapes of Particles

In earlier chapters dealing with the back-scattering by water and ice particles, it was assumed that the drops and stones were spheres. It is known, however, that many types of frozen precipitation differ greatly from spheres. For example, ice crystals and snowflakes are more nearly shaped like flat plates. Small drops usually are close to spheres, but large ones (that is, greater than about 3 or 4 millimeters) are shaped more nearly like a hamburger bun than a base-ball. The bottom surfaces are flattened while the upper surfaces are rounded. Careful photographs of large drops show that they oscillate along a vertical axis as they fall. A drop may flatten out to the point where its vertical dimension is perhaps one-quarter of its horizontal diameter and then bounce back to a rounder shape.

A number of scientists, particularly David Atlas, Milton Kerker, and Walter Hitschfeld, have demonstrated that the nonspherical shapes of the particles affect their back-scattering properties. They restricted themselves to water and ice spheroids much smaller than the radar wave length.

In general, randomly oriented, nonspherical water drops will give a stronger reflected signal than spherical particles of the same mass. If, instead of being randomly oriented, the egg-shaped ones, for example, were arranged with their long axes pointing predominantly in one direction, the returned signal could be either greater or smaller than the signal from spheres of the same mass. The results depend on the character of the electromagnetic wave. Let us look into this problem briefly and return to the eggs and base-balls in a moment.

An electromagnetic wave is produced by causing an electric current to surge back and forth along the length of an electrical conductor. The moving electric charge produces electric fields and magnetic fields. The two fields reach maximum values, go to minima and return to maxima at the frequency (f) of the current surges. Transmitting antennas of all types of radio, television, and radar sets operate essentially in this manner.* They produce fields that oscillate with a predetermined frequency f. As the fields propagate outward, the spacings between the maxima are equal to the wave lengths of the radio waves. As noted in an earlier chapter, the wave length equals the speed of light c divided by the frequency f.

When we speak of an electric field, we refer to a force field that is created in a region between two charged bodies. In the case of the antenna, charges of opposite sign at opposite ends of the conductor create the field. We know that a force exists because when we put a charged object in the field the object moves in a predictable manner. In the same way we establish the force field we call the gravitational field. If we release a stone in the air, it falls to the ground because of the effects of gravity. An electric field is similar in many respects. We cannot see it, but we can establish its presence by noting its effects on charged objects.

A magnetic field is created around a conductor when a current is flowing. You can show that the field exists if you hold a compass in the vicinity of the conductor; the orientation of the compass will change.

A common property of all fields of the type dis-

* In Chapter 2 we discussed the effects of the large metal reflectors used on radar antennas. These reflectors do not create electromagnetic waves. Instead, they act to focus into a beam the energy created by small antennas of the type described here. The conductor producing the radio waves is one-half wave length long and is placed near the focal point of the metallic "dish."

cussed here is that they exert forces in certain specific directions. Gravity exerts a force toward the center of the earth. An electric field exerts forces along the direction of the conductor, while a magnetic field ex-

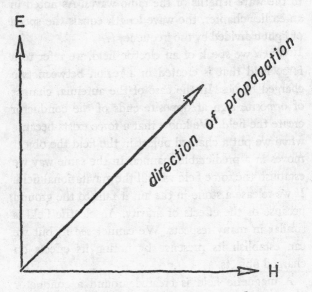

FIG. 20. *An electromagnetic wave can be represented as an electric field, E, and a magnetic field, H, which are perpendicular to one another and which are both perpendicular to the direction in which the wave is moving.*

erts forces directed perpendicularly to the conductor. When describing these fields, it is necessary to refer to the direction of the fields. An electromagnetic wave consists of linked electric and magnetic fields perpendicular to one another, and, as shown schematically in Fig. 20, both fields are perpendicular to the direction in which the wave is moving.

When one considers the back-scattering of the egg-shaped particles whose axes are predominantly in one direction, it is essential to know the direction of the electric field. If the direction of the electric field is the same as the long axis of the egg, the reflection from the particles will be greater than that from spheres of the same mass. If the electric field is perpendicular to the long axis, the reverse is true.

It has been found that the effects of particle shape are less important with particles composed of ice than they are with water particles. As a matter of fact, for most weather problems the shape effects are small and can be neglected, but not always.

In order to explain completely the bright band discussed in Chapter 6, it is necessary to consider the shape of the snow particles. Shape is significant here because the bright band occurs just below the level where the snow particles melt. Although the shape effects are small with dry snow particles, a thin layer of water causes them to behave more nearly like water particles.

An interesting property of nonspherical particles is that when they are randomly oriented relative to the radar antenna, they may act to cause a rotation of the scattered electric field. If the outgoing electric field is horizontal, the returned electric field may be tilted off the horizontal. The amount of the tilt depends on how nonspherical the drops are. With spheres there is no tilting at all, but with egg-shaped particles it would depend on the ratio of the long axis to the diameter. By measuring the tilt or, more correctly, the rotation of the electric field component of the electromagnetic wave, it is possible to make estimates of the shape of the back-scattering particles.

Turbulence in Clouds

In Chapter 5, when discussing the use of radar for measuring rainfall, we indicated that it is necessary to measure the *average received power*. It was pointed out also that because of the movement of the drops, the signal returned from a rainstorm was constantly changing. A number of investigators, particularly Aaron Fleisher and Walter Hitschfeld, have studied the possibilities of making use of the fluctuating characteristics of the signals. They reasoned that if the movements of the drops cause the fluctuations, it should be possible by measuring the fluctuations to draw inferences about the movements.

It is possible to list the factors affecting the motion of the drops. They are (1) gravity, which causes the drops to fall toward the earth at velocities which, in general, increase as the drop diameter increases, and (2) the turbulent motions of the air, which cause the drops to move from side to side or which change the vertical velocity of the drops. Sometimes a steady horizontal movement of the drops can cause a fluctuation of the radar signal, but this effect can be virtually eliminated by employing a radar set with a narrow beam.

After many years of research, Fleisher and his associates have developed an instrument that automatically measures the signal fluctuations. The output of the instrument can be interpreted in terms of turbulent air velocities. Their work has already yielded some interesting results about the variations of air motions in snow and rain storms.

Some Special Wind Measurements

One of the earliest weather applications of radar was that of measuring winds. It accomplished this job by tracking a radar reflector suspended from a rising balloon.

In 1953, two Australians, J. Warner and E. G. Bowen, devised a new scheme for measuring wind. It consists of dropping small radar reflectors from an airborne vehicle and tracking them as they slowly settle toward the earth. The reflectors they used were bundles of small aluminum strips which were about half as long as the wave length of the radar waves and which were called "window" or "chaff." They were used in World War II as a means of confusing radar operators who were searching for approaching aircraft. When a bundle of chaff is tossed out of an airplane, it breaks up in the air stream and distributes hundreds of reflectors over a small volume. On a radarscope the echo looks like that of an airplane. If one airplane were to drop out a large number of bundles in the correct pattern, the echoes on a PPI would resemble a large squadron of airplanes. This ruse had some success during the war.

The chaff in common use has a fall velocity of about 150 ft/min and therefore can be followed for periods of several tens of minutes before it reaches the ground or before the strips of aluminum spread so widely apart that the echo is hard to pinpoint. As the chaff falls, it is carried horizontally by the wind. By tracking its trajectory, one can calculate the winds at the levels through which it has fallen.

It is simple to measure the pattern of the wind by distributing many bundles of chaff at the same elevation and watching them on a single PPI. In recent years, chaff has been dispensed from rockets at high altitudes in order to obtain wind information in regions of the atmosphere seldom reached by ordinary wind balloons.

CHAPTER 11

CONCLUSION

Over the past fifteen years, meteorologists have learned a great deal about clouds and precipitation. Many of the mysteries of thunderstorms, tornadoes, and cyclones have been uncovered. Radar has played an important role in this progress. Along with the instrumented airplane, capable of making detailed measurements in the free air, radar brought to the hands of atmospheric scientists large quantities of new observations to permit better descriptions of many kinds of weather phenomena.

Another instrumental triumph of the last twenty years, the high-speed electronic computer, has made it possible to solve some of the complex equations that describe atmospheric processes and predict future weather. The computer has helped to unravel problems that would have been completely unmanageable in the forties.

Probably the most important development in meteorology in the last two decades has been the rise in the number of highly competent scientists who have joined in the study of the atmosphere. The great advances in all aspects of this, or any other, science are a measure of the competence of the people involved. In the last few years, with the successful launching of artificial satellites, especially the Tiros series of weather satellites, the atmospheric sciences have received added impetus. As these new techniques solve old questions, they create many new and exciting ones. The need for daring and imagination was never so great, the benefits never so satisfying.

APPENDIX

UNITS OF MEASURE USED IN METEOROLOGY

The following conversion factors make it possible to convert from one system of units to another. The abbreviations used in this book are given in parentheses. Note that the number 10 with a superscript means the number 1 followed by a number of zeroes equal to the superscript. For example, 10^5 means 100,000 and 10^3 means 1000. When the superscript is negative, the number is 1 over 10 to the same power. For example, 10^{-5} means $\frac{1}{10^5}$ or $\frac{1}{100,000}$.

1. Length

$$
\begin{aligned}
1 \text{ statute mile (mi)} &= 5280 \text{ feet (ft)} \\
&= 0.8684 \text{ nautical miles} \\
&\qquad \text{(naut. mi)} \\
&= 1609.3 \text{ meters (m)} \\
&= 1.6093 \text{ kilometers (km)}
\end{aligned}
$$

1 kilometer (km)   = 10^5 centimeters (cm)
                    = 10^3 meters (m)
                    = 3280.84 feet (ft)
                    = 0.6214 statute miles (mi)
                    = 0.5396 nautical miles
                        (naut. mi)

1 meter (m)   = 10^3 millimeters (mm)
                    = 10^2 centimeters (cm)
                    = 3.2808 feet (ft)
                    = 39.370 inches (in)

1 foot (ft)   = 12 inches (in)
                    = 30.48 centimeters (cm)
                    = 0.3048 meters (m)

2. Velocity

1 mile per hour
        (mph)   = 0.8684 nautical miles
                        per hour (knot)
                    = 1.4667 feet per second
                        (ft/sec)
                    = 0.4470 meters per second
                        (m/sec)
                    = 1.6093 kilometers per
                        hour (km/hr)
                    = 88 feet per minute
                        (ft/min)

1 meter per second

$\quad$ (m/sec) = 2.2369 miles per
$\qquad$ hour (mph)

$\qquad$ = 1.9425 nautical
$\qquad$ miles per hour (knots)

$\qquad$ = 3.2808 feet per
$\qquad$ second (ft/sec)

$\qquad$ = 196.850 feet per
$\qquad$ minute (ft/min)

$\qquad$ = 3.6 kilometers per
$\qquad$ hour (km/hr)

3. Pressure

1 millibar (mb) = 0.7500 millimeters of mercury
$\qquad$ (mm Hg)

$\qquad$ = 0.02953 inches of mercury
$\qquad$ (in Hg)

$\qquad$ = 0.01450 pounds per square
$\qquad$ inch (lb/in^2)

1 inch of mercury

$\quad$ (in Hg) = 0.4911 pounds per
$\qquad$ square inch (lb/in^2)

$\qquad$ = 33.864 millibars (mb)

1 standard atmosphere = 1013.250 millibars (mb)

$\qquad$ = 760 millimeters of
$\qquad$ mercury (mm Hg)

$\qquad$ = 29.9213 inches of
$\qquad$ mercury (in Hg)

$\qquad$ = 14.6960 pounds per
$\qquad$ square inch (lb/in^2)

4. Temperature conversion formulas

Centigrade degrees (C)
Fahrenheit degrees (F)

$$C = \frac{5}{9} \times (F-32)$$

$$F = \frac{9 \times C}{5} + 32$$

Examples: (1) Temperature $= 50°F$

$$C = \frac{5}{9}(50-32) = \frac{5}{9}(18) = 10°C$$

(2) Temperature $= -10°C$

$$F = \frac{9}{5}(-10) + 32 = -18 + 32 = 14°F$$

ADDITIONAL READING

L. J. BATTAN, *Radar Meteorology*, University of Chicago Press, 1959, 161 pp.

J. S. MARSHALL and W. E. GORDON, "Radiometeorology," in *Meteorological Monographs*, American Meteorological Society, Vol. 3, 1957, pp. 73–113.

J. S. MARSHALL, W. HITSCHFELD, and K. L. S. GUNN, "Advances in Radar Weather," in *Advances in Geophysics*, Academic Press, 1955, pp. 1–51.

These publications listed above give a more advanced and more detailed discussion on the use of radar in meteorology.

G. E. DUNN and B. I. MILLER, *Atlantic Hurricanes*, Louisiana State University Press, Baton Rouge, La., 1960, 326 pp.

A thorough book on all aspects of hurricanes written by two Weather Bureau authorities. Suitable for students and scientifically inclined laymen.

H. R. BYERS, *General Meteorology* (Third Edition), McGraw-Hill Book Co., New York, 1959, 540 pp.

An introductory text for serious students of meteorology.

B. J. MASON, *The Physics of Clouds*, Oxford University Press, 1957, 481 pp.

A comprehensive and detailed account of all aspects of the physics of clouds, precipitation, and thunderstorm electricity.

L. J. BATTAN, *The Nature of Violent Storms*, Science Study Series, S 19, Doubleday, 1961, 158 pp.

A popular discussion of the properties of thunderstorms, tornadoes, hurricanes, and cyclones.

J. F. REINTJES and G. T. COATE, *Principles of Radar* (Third Edition), McGraw-Hill Book Co., New York, 1952, 985 pp.

A book intended primarily for those interested in the basic concepts and techniques of radar. For maximum value the reader should have some knowledge of electronics and calculus.

Weatherwise, American Meteorological Society, 45 Beacon Street, Boston, Mass. Six issues per year.

A journal for students and laymen. It contains short articles on all aspects of the weather, including reports dealing with radar observations. Articles are written in popular terms by experts. This is an excellent means of keeping up to date on the latest weather advances.

INDEX

SCIENCE STUDY SERIES

3604